Touring
on a
Folding Bike

A manual on bike touring
with folding bikes

GIANNI FILIPPINI

FIRST PRINTING EDITION, 2021

ISBN 9798503180923

FRONT COVER IMAGE BY GIANNI FILIPPINI

PHOTOGRAPHY BY GIANNI FILIPPINI

IN GRATITUDE TO SIMON STOTT FOR
CORRECTING THE ORIGINAL MANUSCRIPT

WWW.BROMPTONTRAVELER.COM

Table of Contents

~ PART I ~

Preface

The idea to write this book was not something that came to me suddenly but rather the result of many cycling journeys that were taken over the last ten years. Some were more memorable than others, they all had their highs and their lows, but by the end of each one of them, I never felt disappointed because they always taught me something. Along those roads, lessons were learnt about the way I was riding, the setup I used, how I coped with unexpected events, the stuff I was carrying, bike repairs; of course a lot was learnt about myself.

Being the sort of person who likes to keep organised and take notes, I thought it would be worthwhile to keep track of what worked best and what didn't as a way to improve things in the future, making the next tour even more enjoyable. Doing so meant that the end of each trip was the springboard for a new one, with fresh ideas that could be tested and applied in practice. Like all learning this is a process that continues to this day rather than something to be achieved. I would never have the conceit to suggest that the way I do it is the right one, let alone the only one, but what I can say is that what will be described in this book has worked well for me.

Many books have been written giving instructions and offering suggestions on bicycle travel. You might ask yourself what is different about this one.

Having traveled on a folding bike for several years, the aim is to provide a manual that explains how traveling on a folding bike is not only possible as an alternative to more traditional touring bikes but can also open up a host of new opportunities to discover places in ways you weren't able to before. The most rewarding aspect of sharing my experience on social media is reading how some of my journeys have been able to inspire cyclists, travelers or a bit of both, to one day set off on their own first adventure, and also hearing how much they enjoyed it.

I hope that some of the ideas I share here will help you to find out what works best for you. Following the example of others who have done it before us, is a good way to learn faster than would otherwise be possible. Furthermore, I hope that this reading will be able to offer a new perspective on bike touring that might appeal to all those who are more interested in the discoveries that traveling can bring rather than in achievements and performance. Whether I am fast or slow doesn't really matter that much to me; what I care most about is enjoying the journey pedal stroke after pedal stroke, hopefully learning something in the process too.

~ Ladakh, INDIA (2018) ~

~ California, USA (2013) ~

Introduction

I have always loved cycling in all its different forms. From the rickety bicycle with a pedal brake on which I first learnt to ride, I moved to mountain bikes when they first appeared in the Alps where I used to live. It was the mid 80s and I remember the joy of not being limited to good roads and tarmac and setting off on exciting mountain trails.

A few years later I was craving a flashy Bianchi racing bike that took me up and down the mountains that were around me and on longer rides, through alpine valleys. One thing I remember not being able to make any sense of, were the bunches of cyclists, then mostly Germans, whom I used to see cycling on bikes loaded with bags in the summer. Most of them were heading towards Lake Garda nearby, whilst some of them were surely going even further south, into my country.

I looked at their efforts, pushing such heavy weights, when a plane, car or train would have done it much faster; it all seemed a bit of a mystery. Why so much unnecessary suffering, I wondered? I suppose like most teenagers, all that mattered to me was speed and fitness, and little interest was paid to what one was cycling past. Then, I was completely unaware of the freedom that traveling on a bicycle can provide.

All this changed as an adult when I found out that cycling is the best way to discover and know a region or an entire country, mostly because it doesn't cut you off from your surroundings. You are neither looking at scenery through the windows of an air-conditioned car, nor are distracted by the noise of an engine as you speed past on a motorcycle. The latter would surely feel much more secure and comfortable but at what price?

On a bicycle you are totally exposed, soaked in each sight and scent, at one with and immersed in your surroundings. Only walking can give a similar sense of freedom and reward, but then a bike can enable you to cover longer distances while still relying only on the strength of your body. I find that there is more to it than simply discovering the landscape in a more intimate way. As a cyclist, no matter where you happen to travel to, you will mostly be perceived as approachable and not as threatening.

In my experience I have witnessed how places that are judged unsuitable for traditional tourism or even deemed unfriendly, have a generous welcome for cyclists. Unlike motorists, you are much more likely to be welcomed by strangers who will often want to talk to you, find out where you are coming from and how far you are going. A cyclist, unlike a tourist in a rental car or on a package tour, is never the target of unwanted sales or scams that can sometimes taint the experience of an entire journey and perception of a country.

Exploring our surroundings on a bicycle is also one of the simplest and most accessible ways to set off on an adventure. Whether it is our first weekend ride or a long expedition it doesn't really matter.

If there is some affinity with this magical yet so simple means of transport, deciding to travel in this way, maybe for the first time, will likely uncover the joys it can bring to both our bodies and our minds.

Whether the cycling itself is the main purpose of your journey or the bicycle becomes simply a tool that allows you to make new discoveries, I am confident of one thing. You will experience the possibility of a different way to travel. There might be a few challenges to deal with along the way, there will be moments of pure joy and other times when you will feel frustrated, but by the end of it you will know that it was all well worthwhile.

~ My first Brompton (Bronte) ~

~ My second Brompton (Brutus) ~

How to use this book

In order to present the material in a logical and easy to follow way, after introducing the specific qualities of folding bikes in general, I have tried to follow the process that is involved when a newcomer is interested in planning for his first journey. Despite having in mind a person taking their first steps in the exciting world of bike touring, each section tries to consider all the crucial points that I have found helpful after years of experience.

We all continuously learn how to improve on things, and often this comes from others' suggestions as well as from trial and error. As such I hope that even the more experienced travellers might find some of the material presented useful, or at least that it offers a different perspective to be pondered. It would make sense to follow the book in the order it is presented even though each section can be used and referenced independently according to what is of most interest. Also, despite sharing my personal experience using a folding bike, a lot of the principles found here are transferable to touring on any kind of bicycle.

Not knowing how fit you might be, the type of travel you like, your financial means and maintenance skills, has meant that a beginner's approach has also been a good way to include as many scenarios as possible, making the book useful to most people. If I have been successful in doing so by the end of it, you should have acquired enough knowledge to tackle your first bike touring challenge with a good level of confidence, able to avoid the most common pitfalls that can easily beset the less experienced.

For those who would like to make use of it, I have included a downloadable version of a *'Route Planner'*. This is a Google Sheets document that I use when planning my own tours. You will find a link to download your own copy in the Resources section at the end of this book.

SOUTH OF ENGLAND

DATE			NOTES	STAGE	KM
17 Apr 2021	✈		New York - London (Flight # AA12 Dep: 08:00 Arr: 20:30)	Arrival in London	
18 Apr 2021	🚲	1		LONDON - DORKING	49
19 Apr 2021	🚲	2		DORKING - WINCHESTER	88
20 Apr 2021	🚲	3	AirBnb reservation (tel. 1234 5678910)	WINCHESTER - BOURNEMOUTH	75
21 Apr 2021	🚲	4		BOURNEMOUTH - BURTON	82
22 Apr 2021	🚲	5		BURTON - TEDBURN	106
23 Apr 2021	🚲	6	Hotel Seaview (res # 11223 tel. 1234 5678910)	TEDBURN - PLYMOUTH	91
24 Apr 2021	🚲	7		PLYMOUTH - PENTEWAN	75
25 Apr 2021	🚲	8	Stay at David's place (tel. 1234 5678910)	PENTEWAN - PENRYN	52
26 Apr 2021	⛴		Rest day in Penryn (Ferry excursion)		
27 Apr 2021	🚲	9		PENRYN - LAND'S END	85
28 Apr 2021	🚲	10	AirBnb reservation (tel. 1234 5678910)	LAND'S END - WADEBRIDGE	77
29 Apr 2021	🚲	11		WADEBRIDGE - COOKBURY	89
30 Apr 2021	🚲	12		COOKBURY - DULVERTON	100
1 May 2021	🚲	13		DULVERSTON - GLASTONBURY	99
2 May 2021	🚲	14	AirBnb reservation (tel. 1234 5678910)	GLASTONBURY - BATH	54
3 May 2021	🚆		Bath to London train (dep 12:20 arr 14:00)		
4 May 2021			Sightseeing in London		

~ Route Planner (Calendar) ~

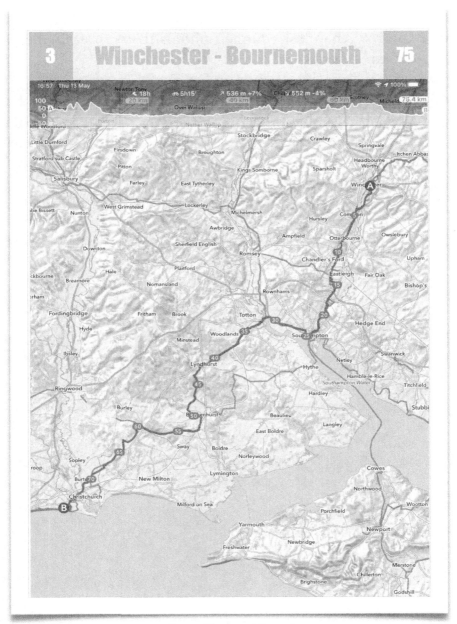

~ *Route Planner (Stage)* ~

PACKING LIST

BIKE	#	CLOTHES	#	CLOTHES	#
Bike	1 ☐	Merino Baselayer	2 ☐	Shoes	1 ☐
Bike Bag	2 ☐	Zip Off Trousers	2 ☐	Flip Flops	1 ☐
Bike Tools	1 ☐	Cycling Trousers	1 ☐	Gore Text Jacket	1 ☐
Bike Lock	1 ☐	Underpants	2 ☐	Woollen Hat	1 ☐
Bike Oil	1 ☐	Socks	2 ☐	Brim Hat	1 ☐
Seat Bar	1 ☐	Shirts	2 ☐	Woollen Gloves	1 ☐
Spare Tyres	1 ☐	Sweater	1 ☐	Cycling Gloves	1 ☐
Spare Tubes	2 ☐	Down Jacket	1 ☐	Long Johns	1 ☐
T-Bag	1 ☐	Light Rain Jacket	1 ☐	Helmet	1 ☐

DOCUMENTS	#	GADGETS	#	OTHERS	#
Passport	1 ☐	Mobile Phone	1 ☐	Tent	1 ☐
Wallets	2 ☐	Go Pro	1 ☐	Matiress	1 ☐
Travel Tickets	1 ☐	Powerbank Battery	1 ☐	Pillow	1 ☐
Credit Cards	2 ☐	Phone Gimbal	1 ☐	Sleeping Bag	1 ☐
Identity Card	1 ☐	Tripod	1 ☐	Silk Liner	1 ☐
Fake Cards	1 ☐	Selfie Stick	1 ☐	Zip Ties	1 ☐
Cash	1 ☐	Torch	1 ☐	Small Lock	1 ☐

~ Route Planner (Packing List) ~

RESERVATIONS

✈ **Transport**

Number	Date	From	To	Reservation #	Dep	Arr
AA 12	17 Apr	LHR	JFK	#42423424	10:30	20:30
AA 13	6 May	JFK	LHR	#42482229	17:00	18:00
GWR Train	3 May	Bath	London	#9345945	12:20	14:00

🛏 **Accomodation**

Hotel	From	To	Reservation #	Phone	Address
AirBnB	20 Apr	21 Apr	#933394	12304 2398423	22 Great Meadow Rd, Bournemouth BH1 1AW
Hotel Seaview	23Apr	24 Apr	#933990	05133 34444	20 Seaview Road, Plymouth
AirBnB	28 Apr	29 Apr	#6345454	01122 445566	7 Rupert Close, Wadebridge PL27 6DP

~ Route Planner (Reservations) ~

Folding Bicycles

Why buy a folding bike?

Before we move to the specific aspects of touring which are what this book is mostly concerned with, let's quickly go over the obvious reasons why nowadays there is a growing interest in folding bicycles. For a start, more and more people spend their working lives in busy cities where space is at a premium and public transport, although convenient, can also be very slow and crowded. In such a common environment, for someone that enjoys cycling, a compact folding bike can be the best compromise and an ideal solution.

If we start considering the smaller living spaces that are common in downtown cities the first problem that you might encounter with a larger bicycle is where to store it when you are not riding it. If you are lucky enough to have some spare garage space this might solve the problem, but if you haven't you will have to lock it somewhere and have trust in your neighbours. On the other hand, you might decide to take it inside your apartment: not an impossible task, but a large bike is definitely more cumbersome to carry around corridors, elevators and staircases in order to access it. It will inevitably take away some valuable space wherever you decide to store it.

A folding bicycle partially solves such inconveniences. If well designed, it folds up small and compact in order to be carried easily and it won't mess up your clothes while doing so. Its small footprint will fit in any little corner or storage room and won't take up that much space even when stored by your entrance door. The same benefits apply to your workplace. If you are working from an office, a regular bike will have to be locked outside and you will be left to worry, hoping you will still find it at the end of a long day. A folding bike is much easier to bring inside, fitting neatly under your desk for example.

Maybe you live a little further away from the centre and from your workplace. Now you might have more living space at your disposal but a longer commute that might take too long to cycle. Whether you drive to work, take a bus or take a train, a folding bicycle could again be the best compromise. You could combine a commute to work with your passion by taking the train for a few stops to get you closer and then cycling for the remainder of the journey. After all a bicycle is easily the quickest way to move fast through the worst downtown traffic.

My final consideration might seem counter-intuitive. I find that a folding bicycle with smaller wheels and a more compact frame makes for an easier ride that feels more secure when dealing with city traffic. Whether this is true or just down to preference is of course debatable. I suggest that, especially for those who are not experienced cyclists but rather commuters electing to use a bicycle, a smaller frame where your feet can easily reach the ground when necessary, can make you feel more secure when dealing with the stop and start traffic of inner cities.

Finally, another common reason why people consider this type of bicycle is the ability to easily pack it and take it along on any kind of trip: it can be such a useful accessory. Whether it is a family weekend at a campsite or a summer holiday, it is easy to find a small space to squeeze one into the boot of a car for example.

Touring on a folding bike

What is the hardest thing about bicycle touring?

Believe it or not, it is not all the pedaling that you have to do!

Ask this question to any cyclist with some experience and the answer will likely be the difficulty in transporting the bike. Each time some sort of transportation is needed, whether it is taking it to the starting point of your chosen destination or bringing it back once the holiday is over, it is anything but stress free. For a start you have to find a large cardboard box to pack the bike into and go through the struggle to lug it to an airport or a train station. Once there you realise that this is only the beginning.

What comes next is trying to convince the check-in staff at the counter to accept your large package without charging you extortionate fees. Rules about the acceptance of bikes on public transport vary from country to country and often change at the last minute. Sooner or later you will probably find yourself in a situation when it is impossible to take the bike with you, perhaps on a train or on a bus journey, while a lift in a car or taking a taxi may also be out of the question due to the lack of space. When it comes to airlines, on a long haul flight a few will accept it without charge, others will charge you a fee for sporting equipment while, should you need a shorter connection on a low cost airline, you will likely be confronted by luggage limitations that will cost you as much as the initial fare.

This is the main reason why, many years ago, I decided to give folding bikes a try.

At first my main concern was to do with quality and reliability. Folding bikes have traditionally served one purpose: short commutes in crowded cities where storage space is at a premium and public transport does not allow access to regular bikes. In the past, they were not considered a viable option for the 'serious' cyclist. To appeal to the casual commuter they had to be good value for money. Reliability was not an issue when they were mostly intended for inner cities where a bike shop, if needed, was never too far away. Riding comfort was also not exactly a priority as most commutes to and from work would not involve long hours spent on the saddle. They were certainly never meant for bike touring or for venturing too far.

In recent years this has changed. The folding bike market has expanded and together with this has come an increased range of bicycles that spans a wide variety of uses and prices. It is now possible to purchase a 'folder' that is both comfortable to ride and sturdy, with components whose quality can compete with its big brothers. Indeed nowadays some folding bikes are even built specifically with touring in mind.

Like with most things there are some trade-offs. While it is possible to push a good folding bike beyond what it was intended for, I believe there are four criteria worth considering before you decide to tour on one; if these don't seem too much of a limitation, I would have no hesitation in recommending this option.

1. <u>You are planning a tour on mostly surfaced roads.</u>

2. <u>You are not planning an extended tour.</u>

3. <u>You will not be touring in extreme temperatures.</u>

4. <u>You will not be in a remote location for any extended time.</u>

(1) Good quality folding bikes are sturdy and can withstand more abuse than you might imagine, but they still mostly use 16" or 20" wheels and thin tyres that are not suited to rough and rocky terrain and perform poorly on muddy trails. I have at times cycled on unpaved roads and been able to cope with the odd exception, but it sometimes meant having to push the bike and walk. If these are the prevalent conditions you will encounter, an expedition touring bike or a mountain bike would be a far better choice. Muddy terrain is also something that folding bikes are not particularly good at. The low clearance of their mudguards and limits on the choice of available tyres make for an uncomfortable ride and could increase your chances of having an accident or taking a fall.

(2) This might be a bit more arbitrary and you can probably prove me wrong, but I have found that for a folding bike luggage setup to work well, it has to be compact and light. You will not be able to carry as many things as you would on a bike with larger wheels and multiple racks. Besides, loading a folding bike to the brim defies the purpose and convenience of the bike in the first place. A bike tour lasting many consecutive months usually involves carrying much more equipment. Furthermore, folding bikes usually have proprietary components that are not easy to source while you are away. An extended tour would inevitably increase the chances that some parts might fail. Depending on where you are touring, such failures could risk spoiling your most careful plans.

(3) Similarly, traveling in freezing temperatures will also inevitably mean having to carry much more weight and gear along in order to be comfortable. Each kilogram of weight you add to your setup will put further strain on the frame and make it harder to carry when other transport is needed. Folding bikes, due to the small wheel circumference, are generally much more responsive and have a twitchy feel about them. With experience, this is something you become adjusted to and learn to compensate for but should you encounter frost and slippery roads, they become even harder to handle. If on the other hand, you plan to tour in extremely hot and dry conditions, you might face another problem. If touring an area where storing large quantities of water is a must to guarantee your safety, a folding bike might not be impossible to use but is not ideal. Due to the folding system and the compact frame, they usually provide only limited attachments for water bottles if any. You can of course store water in your luggage or become creative and strap bottles somewhere else, but weight, maintaining a good balance and space will impose more limitations.

(4) As we have discussed in point 2, folding bikes are also prone to wear and tear and failures during a tour. While touring extensively in remote locations, it is important to be as self sufficient as possible. Given that those proprietary parts can also fail, this means carrying along those spares that you may not otherwise find. In a remote location and off the beaten track, the consequences of having a technical issue that you cannot fix and that prevents you from continuing your ride, could be severe. Help with transportation might not be readily available and your only option is a long walk to the nearest village or town. Traveling in remote areas involves carrying large quantities of water, food, gear and all the gadgets and tools that make it more comfortable and possible. This again, is not as easy on a smaller bike.

As far as reliability and comfort are concerned, my experience is limited to Brompton bikes, but I believe most good quality folders nowadays will guarantee a similar experience. I have toured for about a decade on my Brompton, covering almost 20000 kilometres so far. During all my touring, I have had hardly any reliability issues to report. I can say with some confidence that had I cycled on a mountain bike or a dedicated touring bike, I would have probably experienced much of the same. All I had to cope with mostly were punctures and a few tyre replacements. What is different and extremely important with folding bikes, is to put some extra effort into their maintenance and ensure that they are well tuned and fully functioning before you leave. This is because, unlike regular mountain bikes or more traditional touring bikes, fixing a folding bike involves specific spare parts and different skills that are not always easy to source while traveling. I never depart on a tour without having my bike properly checked and serviced. It means spending a little more money, but my strategy here is to be more proactive than I would be if I were using a standard bike; this has served me well so far. I regularly replace parts that need changing when they exceed their recommended mileage. The chain is swapped when stretched, new gear cables and brake cables are also fitted every few years, to limit the possibility of failures. I am always mindful that I might not be able to source spare parts from local bike shops while I am away. Something I am also always aware of is the need to be gentler on the bike. While climbing a steep hill I refrain from the temptation of standing on the pedals and rocking the bike sideways as I would do on a mountain bike or a racer. When the road gets bumpy or uneven, I ride in a very conservative way and do not hesitate to dismount and take a little walk if I believe it is safer for myself and the bike.

The great benefits in portability mean that you have to make small compromises in comfort, although these are less noticeable than you might think. On my bicycle I have only six gears. It is a simple setup that is enough to climb most mountains where gradients are not too extreme and that has allowed me to climb up to 5300 metres, higher than I have ever been with any other type of bike. We have become accustomed to bicycles with thirty or more gears but I have discovered that provided the ratios are well spaced, six gears are more than adequate to cover most terrains, whether you are climbing uphill or pushing on your pedals during a fast descent. Using a folding bike, as already mentioned, will limit the weight you take with you, and this brings its own benefits. A lighter load makes you faster and often as fast as cyclists on dedicated touring bikes you might encounter along the way. You will, and should be, slower on descents where it is important to be aware of rolling on small wheels, being extra cautious and focused. Your pace and the daily distances you are able to cover will not fall much below those of other cyclists on more traditional setups. There might be times when the road is too steep and you need to break your cycling with a short walk, but I turn this limitation into an advantage. It becomes a good chance to relax a little by using different muscles. On a side note, I have also discovered that a folding bike is rather more comfortable and easier to push.

To conclude, I find that a folding bike is ideal if you are happy to shift the balance from cycling where performance, mileage and speed are important to you, to cycling that is more leisurely and focused on the discovery of a town, a region or even an entire country at a slower pace. Personally, these compromises have been well worthwhile and I haven't looked back since. A decade later, despite owning a larger touring bike, I still find myself using a Brompton as my default bicycle whenever I need to discover a new place and my time is limited to only a few days or a few weeks.

~ Tanglang La, India (5328 m) ~

~ Baralacha La, India (4850 m) ~

~ Babusar, Pakistan (4175 m) ~

~ Monarch Pass, United States (3447 m) ~

29

Multi-Modal touring

Having mentioned some of the pros and cons of folding bicycles, I would now like you to consider maybe the greatest advantage and something which wasn't apparent to me at first. I like to call it 'multi-modal' touring. While a standard touring bike is the best choice for long expeditions or a tour that you will ride all the way from start to finish, a folding bike allows you the flexibility to include several forms of transportation as part of your tour. With a folding bike, in just a few minutes you are able to switch from a fully loaded bicycle to a packed setup that you can hold in your hands and carry on a car, bus, train or plane with extreme ease. It is then possible, should you so wish, to explore the most scenic roads or parts of a country, while bypassing the less interesting ones using other means of transport. **(fig. 13)**

While we all envy cyclists who can afford a gap year and set off on a lengthy world tour, for the great majority bike touring involves taking a shorter holiday break from one's work schedule. Whether you can allow one, two or three weeks, you will want to make the most of the time you can afford to take off. On a regular touring bike you will choose a route that will be of interest to you; if you are well prepared and have done some prior research, most of it will be enjoyable and interesting to ride. Despite this, there will also be the inevitable days when you will be cycling through less interesting stretches, or have no other option than to cycle through heavy traffic putting yourself at risk.

~ (fig. 13) ~

Often, the constraints of time will force you to set priorities and you will have to decide which parts of a country you can visit and which ones you will have to sacrifice.

Let me give you a personal example from a past experience I had, touring on a mountain bike. The destination I had chosen was Japan, a country I had always wanted to visit. As I also loved bike touring I had no doubt that I wanted to have the unique experience of exploring it with my bicycle. Being in full-time work meant that I could afford to take a three week holiday. After a little planning it was clear that if I wanted to visit the four different main islands and all the places I would have liked to see, I had only a few options available.

Taking a series of domestic planes was not viable due to the expense involved but also the risk of damaging the bike each time. Taking a bike on a Japanese train could only be done by packing the bike in a plastic bag and removing the front wheel to make the footprint smaller. If I wanted to use a Shinkansen, the fast and convenient trains the country is famous for, they didn't have a dedicated bicycle storage area, and one had to find a suitable space making sure that it was not in anybody's way. Bear in mind that beyond the mountain bike, I had a couple of large pannier bags and a small front bag in order to carry all my luggage. In hindsight, space for luggage turned out to be really limited on what were always extremely busy trains. I thought about buses too. They were a more economic way to travel around the country but reading about experiences of cyclists at the time it was clear that similar rules to trains applied. On the main tourist routes space was limited and the bike would have had to be partially dismounted and packed in a bag each time. The best option to easily transport the bike was offered by ferries where you could wheel your bike on without any trouble. After some research I figured out that these were too slow to take me where I wanted to go and furthermore, I had to travel to specific ports which were at times not convenient to reach if I followed my plans.

The final decision was to make the most of Honshu, the main island, keeping transfers to a bare minimum. I did take a local train from the airport in Tokyo towards Nikko and a Shinkansen from Osaka to Tokyo on the way back. Both these journeys proved really stressful. I had to carry the packed bike and the rest of my luggage across large stations, through endless corridors, up and down staircases and long platforms. Being in large cities in such a highly populated country, meant that I was struggling to squeeze into small spaces in jam packed train carriages. The cycling itself was enjoyable but at times I had no choice but to go through less interesting places in order to follow the route I had planned. At one point in the Japanese Alps, I encountered a series of really long tunnels which I had to cross by slowly pushing the bike on a narrow side pavement while breathing fumes.

Had I traveled like I do now with my folding Brompton, everything would have been so much easier. With the ability to fold the bike small and pack it fast in an easy to carry bag, I could have planned for a tour that included several train transfers and maybe even a few buses. This would have allowed me to spend some time in Hokkaido, Kyushu as well as visiting some of the sights of the main island that were too far to be reached just by cycling. As far as those tunnels were concerned, had I wanted I could have packed the bike small and hitchhiked a ride to the other side of the mountain, like I once had to do in Zion National Park in Utah.

For some people, bike touring means cycling all the way from the starting point to the end or completing the round of a loop, pedaling every inch of the way. Of course this is a commendable attitude. Most of my tours, even with a folding bicycle, were completed entirely by riding, but there is nothing wrong in having the option to choose what best suits your needs.

I hope I have been able to highlight some of the reasons why cycle touring with a folding bike is not an eccentric endeavour. It can bring noticeable advantages, new opportunities and open up a different way to travel that will shift the paradigm. At times you will be a travelling cyclist, while at other times a traveler who uses his folding bike as a more convenient way to explore. If for you cycling is a tool that helps you to better discover new places, you could find these bikes ideal.

Is it Harder

One of the most common questions I get asked and one of the main concerns is how much more effort is needed to cycle on a folding bike compared to a standard touring bike. This is not surprising. At first sight my Brompton folding bike loaded with luggage at the back and front might look like a harder setup to ride. My usual answer is somehow not satisfying to the questioner:

"It is just a little harder." I would normally say.

I know it is rather a vague reply but it is a simple way to convey my experience over the years. I have extensively toured with mountain bikes and touring bikes in the past. On a folding bike you trade-off a little bit of comfort, but provided you bear in mind the 4 limitations I outlined in the previous chapter, you will hardly tell the difference.

A more interesting question to ask would be:

"Have you felt limited in your ability to tour and explore places by using a folding bike?"

The answer to this question is a resounding no.

If anything, the curiosity to push the boundaries and see how far my Brompton can take me, has pushed me further and I have been able to complete routes that I would have thought challenging on any other bike. I am not saying that with a touring bike you can't push further, go higher and cover longer distances at a faster pace. Anyone interested in speed and performance should probably not choose a folding bike in the first place. But what about those people, whom I believe are in the majority, who are more interested in experiencing the journey and its sights rather than rushing through them?

I have never intended to set personal records, but let me give you a few examples. While touring, my longest daily mileage ever has been 160 kilometres and it was done on a Brompton. Furthermore the highest mountain I have ever climbed on a bike was Tanglang-La in Ladakh. It was 5300 metres in altitude and - you guessed right - I did it riding my Brompton.

Provided that you avoid, as far as possible, rocky trails or muddy roads where folding bikes perform relatively poorly, the ability to go anywhere is only limited by your willingness to adapt a little and by your mindset.

I am sure there are mathematical formulas that contradict what I have said and will tell you that according to physics, the resistance of a 16" wheel compared to a 26", will make you slower by a certain percentage, but you won't notice this much in practice, and that is all that really matters. Do find a good quality folding bicycle that gives you a comfortable riding position for long hours in the saddle, and your experience will likely confirm what I am saying.

As far as other aspects are concerned that make it marginally harder, I will mention a few in an effort to be as fair and exhaustive as I possibly can.

1. **Aerodynamics:** These will play a part, especially if riding against strong headwinds. You might find that folding bikes encourage you to take a position that is less aerodynamic and thus offers more resistance. This is an aspect that is taken into account mostly whilst racing but I am not denying that a long day facing

strong headwinds can be a challenge. In truth most touring bikes, no matter their size, are mostly set up for a more comfortable ride that you can keep for many hours rather than challenging you in an uncomfortable position. Also, no matter the bike, you will still have all the luggage that makes you slower and is anything but aerodynamic. A touring bike with drop bars could still give you a slight advantage, which takes me to the second point.

2. **<u>Handlebars:</u>** Beyond what is offered as standard on folding bikes, they tend to be smaller and less customisable, since they must fit with the specific folding system of the bike itself. You will probably have more limitations in terms of the hand grips, something you can improve by adding some third party appendixes **(fig. 14)** and the positions your body can take while riding. While touring long hours every day this can contribute to a less comfortable ride overall. When your body position and the ability to change it is limited, it becomes crucial to find a folding bike that is comfortable and fits your body right off the bat because modifying the original set up is usually much harder.

3. **<u>Gears:</u>** There are folding bikes, especially those at the higher end of the market, that offer a wide range of gears, but these usually come at a higher cost. Generally, folding bikes are more limited in the number of gears they offer and less options will mean a harder ride at times. On my Brompton I tour with only six gears, which means that I have less choices to precisely

match the ratios to the terrain I am riding. If this might sound like a great discomfort, I would argue that you do not need 20 or 30 gears as we are now grown accustomed to have. A few gears with well spaced ratios that are soft enough to climb a steep hill and hard enough to push the pedals when descending a mountain are all you need.

These are some of the reasons why a folding bike might be a little harder to ride. Still, they are perfectly capable of managing long and even challenging tours, provided you are willing to make a few small sacrifices for the benefits they can bring.

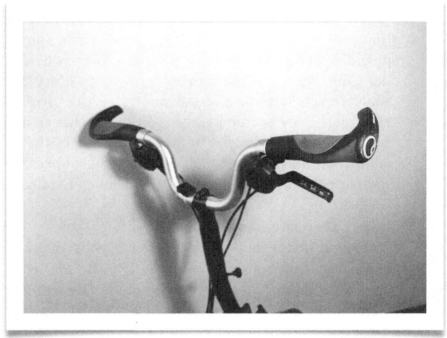

~ (fig. 14) ~

Preparation

Choosing the Right Bicycle

This book is not about recommending a particular bicycle model but what I can do is give you a few hints to help you select what is right for you. To start your search for the ideal folding bike, you might want to have a look at some of the most common quality brands on the market; these include Brompton, Bike Friday, Tern, Birdy, Airnimal and Dahon to name but a few. When I first had to make a choice, I opted for a Brompton bike. It was widely available in England, where I lived at the time, and had a good reputation as a reliable bike that could be used even for touring. After many successful tours I don't regret that choice. Brompton has arguably designed the best and most compact folding system, they have a solid frame and reliable components, as well as one of the smallest footprints on the market.

Reliability is always the main concern when bike touring. Dealing with a technical failure that stops you from continuing your journey can be an annoying and at times stressful experience. Folding bikes are more vulnerable in some ways. To the usual wear and tear and breakdowns that any bike can experience, there is a folding system that adds further complications; added to that, they are not usually built to carry heavy loads and for riding long distances. As we have already discussed, parts are often proprietary and not as easy to source. For these reasons, the build and the quality of the components used becomes even more important than on other bicycles.

~ Brompton ~

~ Bike Friday ~

~ Tern ~

My suggestion then is to invest as much as possible within your budget and to choose the best bike you can afford to buy.

Some of the brands I have mentioned are not particularly cheap. If their price is over your budget, I would rather recommend buying them second hand than choosing models which might be more affordable but are more likely to disappoint you in the long run and spoil your plans. Having said that, folding bikes have a great advantage even when it comes to dealing with a serious breakdown. It is much easier to get a lift from passing cars, buses or trains should it become necessary. If you are willing to take more risks and adapt your plans should things not work out, your budget, whatever it might be, will be enough to make it work for you. Whatever bicycle you choose, I advise you to learn as far as possible how to fix the most common breakdowns you are likely to encounter. The more you can repair yourself, the greater the confidence you will have to tour with the bike, and the greater your peace of mind.

Above all do not let my advice and any budgetary limitations stop you from following your dreams and have fun touring. You will not be the first nor the last person to prove me wrong and successfully tour the world on what is considered a 'cheap' and 'unsuitable' bike. After all, only a century ago, when the choice of bikes was limited, the quality mostly poor and spare parts hard to find, the ingenuity and thirst for adventure spurred countless people to embark on amazing journeys with what they had available.

The Bicycle I Ride

As all my experience touring with a folding bike has been on a Brompton I will now discuss what models are the most appropriate and some of the choices I recommend. When you order a new Brompton you will also be deciding what type of components and accessories you would like for your bike. This process comprises three main parts that will determine the characteristics of your build. The first part relates to the bike's handlebars, the second how many gears you would like to have and the last whether the bike will have a rear rack and be fitted with mudguards.

Handlebar types:

These come in three options that will determine your riding style. The S-type is a flat handlebar that offers the most aggressive and aerodynamic position on the bike. Next option is the M-type and is probably the most common one. It offers a good balanced posture that is a little less aerodynamic but more comfortable. Last option is the H-type bar which is tailored to a more upright and comfortable ride and is more suitable for tall riders.

Gear types:

A standard Brompton ranges from 1 to 6 speed. Single speed is the lightest and simplest version and the cheapest one on offer. As a single speed bike it makes maintenance easier and cheaper, but not having the ability to shift gear and modify your range limits the use of this version to flat terrain. Similarly a 2 speed option is also more targeted to occasional city commutes without hills. The 3 speed model introduces the Sturmey Archer hub gear system. This adds weight to the bicycle but you get 3 well spaced gears that can be shifted even when stationary. Finally Brompton's most versatile gearing option combines two sprockets at the rear with the Sturmey Archer systems, allowing for six well spaced gears. It comes to almost a kilogram of extra weight compared to the single gear option but is still a relatively easy system to maintain.

Mudguards and rear rack types:

This is a simple choice between an E-version with no mudguards and rack, a L-version that comes fitted with mudguards and a R-version that comprises both mudguards and a rear rack.

Brompton does offer other modifications like a lighter version with titanium parts. These do change all the time and tend to be rather expensive for the amount of weight that you are saving.

Having talked about the options you have, the version I have been using and can recommend for touring is what is normally referred to as M6R. The code refers to a model with M-type handlebars, 6 Sturmey Archer gears and rear rack and mudguards fitted.

Other options:

Seatposts:

As the frame has a fixed size the main adjustment depending on your height is the seatpost length. The standard seatpost is for riders with an inside leg of up to 84 cm. If your height fits this option, the saddle can be lowered the most allowing for the most compact fold size. For taller riders with an inseam length over 84 cm an extended seatpost is available. When the bike is folded this will not allow the saddle to be lowered completely, slightly increasing the size of the fold. For taller riders who would like a higher seatpost while still keeping a compact fold, a telescopic post is also available. It is the heaviest option of the three but brings the extra benefit of an easily removable saddle when you pack the bike.

Tyres:

The size of Brompton tyres is 16 x 1 ⅜ inches with an Etrto (European Tire and Rim Technical Organization) of 35-349 mm. Standard tyre models do vary and are changed regularly. At the time of writing Schwalbe Marathon tyres are a common choice among those who tour with these bicycles.

Handlebars:

Finally something I really recommend is to have some sort of grips fitted to the handlebar so that you are able to shift the position of your hands making your posture much more comfortable when you cycle.

Do You Need to Be Fit

It is a common misconception that you need to be particularly fit in order to be able to tour on a bicycle; and this is probably one of the main reasons why it is still a niche activity in the world of travel. It is often imagined to be a gruelling endeavour that demands the physical strength and stamina of a real athlete. This is far from the truth and a little experience in bike touring will confirm this. You will often be approached by strangers you meet on the road who will be full of praise and admiration, as though you had just managed to summit Mount Everest unscathed. This praise is of course welcome and will make you feel proud of what you are doing and encourage and motivate you to continue. Others will be extremely kind to you while at the same time feeling sorry for your plight; they assume that you must be miserable and that only a masochist could be inflicting such pain on their body. Both responses result from that same wrong assumption:

"I could never do what he or she is doing."

If one really looks at cycle tourists, some of them cycling for months or years on expeditions circumnavigating the planet, one mostly finds that they are ordinary men and women who come in all shapes and forms and with varying fitness levels. Yes, there will be a few that are out there to be competitive and to beat records, but for the most part the only concern is to reach the destination for that day, possibly before getting too tired, and to enjoy the ride.

Of course for some unlucky ones, whose poor health hinders making too much effort, cycling might not be an option. For the majority though, cycling offers the opportunity to improve one's fitness, never mind what the starting point is. When done regularly, as on a tour, cycling brings a host of benefits. It promotes weight loss, burns fat while building leg muscle and enhances endurance. Like other aerobic exercises it improves the health of heart and lung functions while being fairly low impact on your body thanks to the lack of weight bearing.

Even if to start with, one is overweight or lacks a good fitness level, these are not essential elements and they shouldn't prevent you from giving bike touring a try. Beyond the simple ability to ride the bike and getting adjusted to the fact that you will be carrying the extra weight of your bags, improved fitness levels will naturally follow. What you also need to take into account is that you are not competing in a race. A bike tour involves going from point A to point B, but only you are deciding how far and how challenging that route should be. Certainly a bike tour can be adapted to fit a wide range of cycling abilities and fitness levels without having to strain.

To begin with, it is a good idea to start with a few test rides to figure out what kind of distances and pace are comfortable for you. Whether you decide to set up a training program to be as fit as possible before you depart is entirely up to you. Crucially if you are not as fit as you would like to be from the start, you shouldn't worry. Of course the fitter you are the longer you will be able to ride each day and the more comfortable you will find it. As you begin the tour, depending on that fitness, there might be some adjustments to be made. Provided you listen to your body fatigue levels during the first few days without overdoing it, your body will adapt and get fitter, gradually adjusting in the process. There is nobody to race against, so it is best to ride at a pace that feels comfortable for you and to take all the time you need to enjoy the journey. Indeed one of the joys of traveling is talking to the people you meet along the way, discovering their culture and getting to know their landscapes.

Before I set off for a tour, I have never found it necessary to train specifically to be better prepared. What I try to do during the year is maintain a relatively good shape and fitness; in my case I do so mostly by some gentle running a few times a week and a longer bike ride a couple of times a month depending on the season. Once on the bicycle, ready to depart, I usually find that while I might struggle a little during the first couple of days, by the third or fourth one I can adjust to the level of effort that is required. Our bodies are incredibly adaptable machines and even if you are not able to train a little before the start, once you begin, your stamina and endurance will grow as you ride and mileage that seemed hard to reach will become perfectly feasible. It is likely that by the end of the trip, you will be surprised at how far you have been able to go, feeling proud of what you were able to achieve on your very first adventure.

Going solo or with others

One of the main decisions to be taken at the start is whether to travel solo, as a couple or in a larger group. This decision will be dictated by your circumstances and preferences. It is good to realise that each option has its own advantages and disadvantages.

Going solo is in many ways the simplest choice. Its main advantages are that it is much easier to decide where, when and how to travel, giving complete control of the overall experience. A bike tour, like a long trek, is a very physical experience and sharing it with others is best done when fitness levels are at least comparable. If you are much slower or faster than people you are touring with, you will have to adapt and make the necessary changes to what feels most comfortable for you.

This is not true for everybody but I find that I can cover greater distances with more ease when cycling on my own. I suppose it relates to the innate ability some have to motivate themselves, while others might need that extra bit of support and encouragement. The larger the group you are riding with, the more times you will be forced to stop and wait in order to stay together. Connected to this is what I would say is the single most important advantage of riding solo, the ability to stop and go whenever you feel like it. The simple fact of being aware that at any moment you can decide to have a meal if you feel hungry, catch your breath when tired or simply allow yourself the time to take in the landscape without inconveniencing others, gives you that peace of mind and independence that ultimately let you ride further.

As a solo rider, whether male or female, you will be more approachable for strangers. A couple or a group tend to stick to one other and this makes it more unlikely that people you meet along the way will join you to chat. There is also an opposite perspective to it. When touring solo you will make more of an effort to strike up a conversation with a person you happen to encounter. In an emergency situation, should you be on your own and need help, it will likely be offered quicker than if you were with another person or a group, as a person on his own is perceived as more vulnerable.

When you are touring on your own, it is generally easier to find accommodation; after all an extra person doesn't need that much space. This might also be true of a couple but then you might have other constraints like privacy that will make it a little harder.

Finally you have also all the freedom to decide if you want to change a certain plan, modify the route or the length of your tour, all things that get much more complicated and need to be discussed and agreed upon when traveling with others.

Is riding solo then the ultimate bliss and ideal way to tour for everybody? Definitely not. Some of us are more introverted and able to enjoy our own company, while for others there is a need for a bonding and sharing that can only be had together.

There will be times when you are on your own and feel that solitude that is sought by some while avoided by others.

Touring on your own is going to be more expensive as you won't be able to share some of the costs. Accommodation in hotel rooms will likely work out much cheaper for couples or groups, as hotels often charge per room rather than per person; similarly costs at a campsite are composed of a fixed charge for the tent spot and a smaller charge for each person that shares it. As a couple, of course, you will only need to invest in one tent and will be able to share the weight of the camping gear between two bikes.

Experience might also play a part in your choice. I wouldn't go as far as saying that a beginner on their first ever tour should not ride solo; however, for some, riding with another person might be a good way to break the ice and overcome the initial fears and hesitations. This will provide reassurance and that extra bit of confidence that you might lack at first.

Finally, an excellent way to find out what bike touring is all about, is to join an organised tour. These can provide an ideal introduction to traveling with a bike while removing the need to spend time in organising all the practicalities. In a group tour you will have the chance to meet like-minded people and share experiences, which will be very useful for future rides. Naturally, organised travels are going to be more expensive as you are relying on the expertise of guides, backup vehicles and support staff that will sort out technical problems, giving you a lift if you are too tired, as well as providing all the food and accommodation. They will usually also take care of most of your luggage, leaving you free to enjoy the cycling without having to carry too much weight. Another attractive side to organized tours is the fact that they rely on the knowledge of local guides who will know the most scenic routes to follow and the best sights. For cyclists who might have some experience with touring but would like to explore a more adventurous type of trip, a group tour removes some of the challenges making any destination more accessible.

Equipment you might need

What I would like to do in this chapter is to go into some detail about the things I carry when touring solo on a folding bike. It will be a detailed chapter based on a tried and tested list of items that I have refined over the years. I hope it will prove useful to those new to touring, but also to those with some experience. I am aware that we all have different needs and levels of comfort we are aiming for while touring on a bicycle. Before going through it item by item, this is the 'Route Planner' Packing List that I generally use. **(fig. 18)**

This list works best as a starting point; beyond that, it will be up to you to assess what is unnecessary and what is missing as you are the best person to make those judgments. Chances are that you will not get this right first time round, but the more experience you gain the better you will become at finding the right balance between comfort and the limits of what you can carry on the bike.

PACKING LIST

BIKE	#	CLOTHES	#	CLOTHES	#
Bike	1	Marino Baselayer	2	Shoes	1
Bike Bag	2	Zip Off Trousers	2	Flip Flops	1
Bike Tools	1	Cycling Trousers	1	Gore Text Jacket	1
Bike Lock	1	Underpants	2	Woollen Hat	1
Bike Oil	1	Socks	2	Brim Hat	1
Seat Bar	1	Shirts	2	Woollen Gloves	1
Spare Tyres	1	Sweater	1	Cycling Gloves	1
Spare Tubes	2	Down Jacket	1	Long Johns	1
T-Bag	1	Light Rain Jacket	1	Helmet	1

DOCUMENTS	#	GADGETS	#	OTHERS	#
Passport	1	Mobile Phone	1	Tent	1
Wallets	2	Go Pro	1	Mattress	1
Travel Tickets	1	Powerbank Battery	1	Pillow	1
Credit Cards	2	Phone Gimbal	1	Sleeping Bag	1
Identity Card	1	Tripod	1	Silk Liner	1
Fake Cards	1	Selfie Stick	1	Zip Ties	1
Cash	1	Torch	1	Small Lock	1
Emergency Card	1	Odometer	1	Bunjee Straps	2
Planner	1	Bike Lights	2	Compression Bags	5
Offline Maps	1	Solar Panel	1	Zip Lock Bags	5
Online Docs	1	Lanyard	1	First Aid Kit	1

~ (fig. 18) ~

There is nothing like setting off on your first tour to highlight the things that you miss and those that maybe you should not have taken and could easily have left behind. Keeping notes as you travel will be an effective way to remember the adjustments that you will need to make the next time. The Packing List contains everything I normally bring on a tour and when I return should there be something to add or remove, I edit it. When the time comes for preparing the next one, I use it and follow it conscientiously. It makes the process of packing much quicker, but most importantly it helps to ensure that nothing is skipped or forgotten.

I have already mentioned that on a folding bike there are more limitations on the things you can carry. You will not be able to carry as much as you can on a fully loaded touring bike. Besides, were you able to find a way to load a lot of stuff on it, you would have done so at the expense of the main practical advantage these bikes give you. With lots of bags strapped onto its frame, even a folding bike won't be easy to fold and to carry on a bus or in a car whenever this becomes necessary. My advice, therefore, is always 'the lighter the better'.

The main variable that will affect this list is the kind of tour you are planning. Whether you are going to tour in a remote region or will be hopping from town to town in a densely populated area will determine what you are likely to need most. Will you be staying in hotels each night or are you intending to spend every night camping in the wild? Are there many facilities along your route, will you be able to source good food frequently or do you need a level of self-sufficiency in what you eat and drink during the day? Thinking about repairs and tools you should carry, this will differ depending on how likely you are to regularly find a bike shop along the way, but also on your ability to carry out specific repairs yourself.

What I am including here is a comprehensive list that enables you to be pretty much self-sufficient on a tour that could last from a short week to a full month. I use it as a reference to prepare everything I need before I leave for a trip. Most of the entries are self explanatory but to avoid possible confusion, I thought it would be a good idea to follow it point by point, describing each item I carry. It is divided into five sections: Bike, Clothes, Documents, Gadgets, Others.

Let's have a look at what is included in the <u>Bike</u> Section:

Bike: Very unlikely that one would forget it but I still put it down as my top item just in case!

Bike Bags: I carry 2 soft bags with me. One is a general soft bike bag with handles and a shoulder strap and the other one a plastic, heavy duty and cheap bag that fits the bike more tightly, in order to further protect it.

Bike Tools: What you will need will vary according to the bike you are traveling with. As a minimum you should carry a good portable pump, a set of spanners and allen keys that fit the different sizes of nuts and bolts of your bicycle, a repair kit for punctures and levers to remove your tyres. If you are able to carry out some more advanced repairs, consider bringing spare brake pads, a few spare spokes and the key to adjust them, as well as a chain removal tool and a few spare links to repair a broken chain. Similarly, bringing spare gear and brake cables can be a good idea. A small portable plier and a swiss army knife is also something very useful to have for those times when the right tool is not available and you need to find some creative solutions. Not exactly tools, but something I recommend carrying is strong packing tape and an assortment of zip ties of different thickness, length and sizes as these can save your day in all kinds of emergencies.

Bike Lock: You will need it to secure the bike each time you have to leave it unattended.

Bike Oil: Bike oil to keep all parts well lubricated

Seat bar: This is only necessary if you intend to use my system to fix a backpack to the rear of a folding bicycle, and that I will explain in a later chapter.

Spare tyres: When touring on a folding bicycle I recommend bringing a spare tyre or two depending on the distance you want to cover. You will find that these tend to wear out quicker due to the small wheels, and should you need a new one a good quality small tyre is always hard to find. Bike shops normally store these sizes mostly for children's bicycles and would not have anything you would be able to use.

Spare inner tubes: Punctures will be the main issue you will likely have to deal with. Do bring some patches and glue to repair tubes, but for convenience I find it a good idea to carry a couple of spare new ones. Should you have a puncture you can swap the damaged one for a new one, shortening the repair time. When you end your day and are in a well sheltered place you can then fix the punctured tube at your leisure with patches and glue so that it can be used the next time.

T-Bag: This is relevant to using a Brompton setup and is the large bag that is clamped to the front of the bike frame. Depending on the folding bike you use and your setup you can substitute this for your second largest bag, in which you will be carrying your luggage.

Next on the list is the <u>Clothes</u> Section. **(fig. 19)**

Let me start by saying that I do not usually bring any cycling-specific clothes, with the exception of a helmet. Sometimes I do bring cycling trousers with padding for extra comfort and I know for some this is a necessary item, and a pair of cycling gloves. For the rest, as you will see, I mostly bring what could be categorized as outdoor, mountaineering or trekking clothing. In my experience these are much more versatile than cycling-specific clothing that is often designed for a day ride rather than for multiple days anyway. Outdoor clothes materials are resistant, durable, breathable, can be waterproof, quick drying and usually much more comfortable to wear, at least for the long days on the bike that any cycling tour requires. The other great advantage is that, unlike cycling gear, they can be worn in all situations, whether on the bike, sightseeing or having a meal at a restaurant.

A common refrain you will hear in this manual is that touring on a folding bike requires you to travel lighter. If you decide to use cycling clothes while cycling you will inevitably end up having to bring also those spare clothes that are more suitable for other situations when you are not on the bike. Before you know it, you will have another bundle of items that while not be necessarily overwhelming in size or even in weight, but will add up to the volume and the demand for space that on your folding bike is precious and quite limited.

DOWN JACKET   GORE-TEX JACKET   TREKKING SHIRT

CYCLING SHORTS

SWEATER

UNDERPANTS

ZIP-OFF TROUSERS

MERINO BASELAYER   SOCKS

WOOLEN HAT   GLOVES   BRIM HAT   LONG JOHNS

~ (fig. 19) ~

Let's have a look in detail at the clothes I bring:

Merino Baselayer: I never travel without some Merino wool shirts with long sleeves that I use as my baselayer. Merino wool, though a little pricey, has some amazing properties that make it ideal for touring and all kinds of outdoor activities. It is softer, therefore more comfortable on your skin, than regular wool, but mostly it is one of the best materials to regulate your body temperature, transport sweat away as vapor and neutralize bad odours. I prefer long sleeves. If it is cold they will keep you warmer; and if it is hot and you are riding under a baking sun, they will prevent your arms, which are always exposed for long hours, from getting sunburnt.

Zip off Trousers: Again, two is the magic number! The idea of having two items is of course in order to be able to have a clean change for those things that you wear more often, and to be able to wash and dry the spare ones. As my main trousers on and off the bike, I like to bring zip off trousers that are normally used for trekking. Without the bottom section they are perfect for cycling and in the evening you can reassemble them and create an elegant outfit. If you are into cutting ounces, you could go as far as buying two of the same type. That way you could bring 2 shorts and only one set of the lower part that will fit on either!

Cycling Trousers: This is one of the exceptions I mentioned. To be perfectly honest I tend not to bring these. I find that if I am touring on a comfortable saddle my rear is just as comfortable without them. There are times when I have taken them and used them, especially at the beginning of the tour, wearing them under my outdoor trousers, to get me adjusted. I am aware that this is a personal preference and that for some cyclists having some padding is essential. See what works best for you. On the plus side they of course provide some padding, but otherwise they bring all the disadvantages of cycling clothes. They are not as comfortable to wear, they are not breathable, they tend to pick up odour much quicker, they stick out like a sore thumb when you are off the bike, and because of the padding, take ages to dry each time you wash them.

Underpants: If you are not using cycling trousers you will need some underpants. Find a light and good material that is comfortable for you and possibly quick to dry. Hygiene is not an issue because you will want to wash them every day anyway, alternating between the two pairs you are carrying. I normally wash the pair I have worn under the shower when I end my day and let it dry at night while wearing the clean one. Even if they are not dry in the morning, you will have plenty of time to dry them on the bicycle, ready and fresh to give you a change at the end of the following day.

Socks: I use Merino wool again for the good breathability and the fact that I am able to wear them for longer. If you are using some type of sandal shoes while you are on the bicycle, your feet are free to breathe and you will find that you can go for a week or more without washing the socks. It sounds gross I know, but it is not that bad!

Shirts: On top of the Merino baselayer I wear a short sleeved shirt. I like trekking polo shirts in a light synthetic material. They usually come in all kinds of colours and patterns and you can choose colours that will disguise the stains and the dust that you inevitably pick up by riding in the open all day. They are elegant enough off the bike and another advantage is that they can have pockets on the chest which you can use to tuck away a snack, easy to access, or even your mobile phone if it fits safely.

Sweater: The best way to adapt to different climates is to wear thin layers. In this layering system, the sweater is your mid layer, ideal for the times when it is too cold to be cycling in your baselayer and shirt only. Choose a sweater that is comfortable, warm and light in weight at the same time. Fleece is a good material that meets all those criteria, but you will have many others to choose from. A sweater is a little harder to wash and bulkier in your luggage. That is why I only bring one. As I might not be able to wash it as often, anything that dries quickly, and is of a darker colour that won't show dirt and stains, will be the perfect candidate.

Down Jacket: This and your rain jacket will be the outer shells of your layering system. A down jacket is excellent to give you that extra warmth if you are touring in colder climes, but also for mornings, evenings and nights. They come in all kinds of weights and sizes. What I bring is the most compact version I can find, sometimes called a 'puffer jacket'. They often come with a pouch to stuff them into, which makes them very small to carry.

Light Rain Jacket: If you are carrying a Gore-tex or other waterproof jacket this is not necessary, but I like to bring one along as they are extremely tiny and fit into one hand. They are easy to put on and take off and can be kept within easy reach for times where you want to protect from the wind on a downhill or a light rain drizzle while you are riding.

Shoes: You will be wearing them all day, on and off the bike, so do select something that is comfortable for you. Of course if you decide to use clip on pedal systems you will have to carry what works with them. Otherwise any trekking shoe that is light, while still providing some stiffness in the sole, is good. My personal favourites are hybrid shoes that are a mix between sandals and trekking shoes. There are several on the market and some of them have the added benefit of being waterproof. This means that should you want, that is the only pair you ever need to bring along with you. A sandal paired with thick socks is ideal. When it is chilly you can wear them with socks, while if you get hot you can wear them with bare feet and that will help you to stay cool. If it rains, unless you are riding in cold temperatures, again you can ride in sandals with bare feet, keeping your socks dry for later. When getting really wet, a sandal is much quicker to dry than an enclosed shoe, and due to the fact that they let your feet breath easily, they are much less likely to get smelly after long wear.

Flip Flops: If you are carrying waterproof sandals you might not need these, but a pair of cheap flip flops gives you the option of having something easy to change into at the end of the day and to use off the bike, especially when camping.

Made of rubber, they are extremely light and won't take up too much space should you want to bring them along.

Gore-Tex Jacket: Gore-Tex has become synonymous with a material that can be breathable and also keep you dry while riding in the rain. Whatever material you decide to buy, remember that keeping dry and warm is essential in the outdoors if the weather turns bad. As we are wearing layers, the issue of waterproofing is the main aspect to think about. Choose a jacket that is also not too heavy, thick and bulky to carry in your luggage. For the coldest rainy days it will just be your top layer and you could wear your down jacket and fleece sweater underneath.

Woollen Hat: I find this is useful for cold conditions and especially if you are intending to camp out some nights. A warm hat will keep you much warmer when camping at night in a sleeping bag.

Brim Hat: I am very partial to brim hats! A brim hat has for many years been a trademark of my tours on a Brompton folding bike. I have to admit being guilty: I have included a cycling helmet on my list, but for most of my touring I have never used one. I wouldn't want to set a bad example though, as I know not wearing a helmet exposes you to more risk should you have an accident, and to some people it is plain stupid not to use one. When questioned about it I always say that it is a risk I am willing to take and that I try to compensate by being extremely careful in the way I ride. As a side note I should add that riding on a folding bicycle needs more care and attention, since the small wheels make it easier to fall should you hit a hole, a rock or some kind of obstacle. Be always focused on the road and do travel slower than you normally would, especially when going downhill.

Woollen and cycling gloves: Your hands, your head and your feet will be the first to get cold. Gloves are small and light enough to carry even when you are not expecting to ride in cold temperatures. Even in mild climates or in summer all that you need is a stint of bad weather or a tall mountain to climb to realise that you were not well prepared.

Long Johns: Not essential, but something I like to bring for the night at the campsite. When necessary they keep you warm while sleeping.

Helmet: For those that still think I am irresponsible... Here it is. This is one of the items that most cyclists would recommend packing - and wearing! Enough said that in a bad fall, should you hit your head, it could make the difference between life and death.

Moving to the Documents Section, I like to keep track of all the documents I need to carry. Use this as a reference, bearing in mind that your personal circumstances and travel destination are important variables.

Passport: Depending on where you are traveling, bear in mind that often at least six months validity is a requirement in many countries.

Wallets: Why do I list 2 wallets you might wonder? Certainly not so that I can wash one at the end of the day! Let me share a secret with you, hoping that you will not cross me on a tour and be tempted to rob me of my belongings... I carry a true wallet and a fake wallet. The true wallet with money and credit cards is stored safely in my front bag that I always remove and take with me when I am away from the bike. The fake wallet is the one I usually handle daily. It contains some cash in local currency but otherwise mostly credit or debit cards that have long since expired. In an emergency, should I fall victim to an attempt to rob me, this is the one I would hand over if I had to. I make sure it always contains some cash, otherwise it might raise some eyebrows!

Cash: Currency that you will need. Depending on where you are travelling to, it can also be useful to carry US Dollars or Euros as a backup. These are usually accepted in many countries and will be easy to exchange wherever you happen to be.

Travel Tickets: Airplane tickets or other tickets that you will need for the journey.

Credit Cards: Real and fake ones! Another useful option are international Debit cards that can be loaded with local currency and used at ATM machines, as well as for payments. The advantage of these is that they have limited funds on them, so even in the unlikely event that a pin is stolen it is not a disaster.

Identity Card: If you own one, otherwise a second document that could be useful to prove your identity. Keep this in a separate location and bag from the passport.

Emergency Card: This is a useful thing to have - and I am not trying to put you off touring, in case you are wondering! It is a small card with my next of kin contact details in case of any emergency. I store it in one of the wallets, hoping that it will never have to be used!

Planner: This is the 'Route Planner' I have already introduced and that you will find linked, so that you can download your own copy with instructions, in the Resources section. It is a digital file I prepare and save in pdf format. It contains my plan for each day, with distance, towns and facilities along the way; phone numbers and contacts I might need; hotels, bed & breakfast or camping places I could stay in, and so on. I like to have things organised and easy to find. Others prefer to take each day as it comes, without too much planning. Should you fall into this category you might find this unnecessary and a waste of time.

Offline Maps: I know there are paper map lovers out there! If they work best for you, invest in good maps of the area you will be visiting. I prefer to go the digital way so that I can have everything I need stored on my phone or tablet.

Online Docs: I keep digital copies, mostly photos, of things such as passport, tickets and other documents I carry. These can be stored securely online by using some kind of cloud service or simply by emailing them to yourself for easy access on a phone or any computer you can access. It is always possible to misplace or lose things as you travel; having a backup digital copy of important documents may not always work, but I think it is a good strategy.

The next category is the <u>Gadgets</u> Section.

This section is very subjective and depends on what you need to do, what you are used to and what you already own. The most useful functions you will need to consider in electronic gadgets are security, navigation, communication, storage and power.

A modern smartphone may be the only thing you need to bring. It can guide you with maps and GPS, keep you in touch with friends and relatives, and allow you to document your trip with videos and photos should you want to. For all the gadgets you are planning to bring, also ensure that you have all relevant cables, chargers, memory cards and props you need to be able to use them and to keep them functioning.

<u>Mobile Phone:</u> Any phone you already use will be perfect. As this is something we rely on more and more in our daily lives, it is even more important when we are traveling. Because of this, if you can take an old phone with you I recommend having it as a backup, maybe storing it in a different place. This is what I do, should anything happen to my main one. As a lot of what I need is stored in the phone memory, I duplicate all the information I need to have it readily available on both phones.

GoPro: There will be a full section on documenting your trip in the Touring chapter where I will go into more detail about what I use and how. An action camera is a good way to document your trip with videos should you want to.

Powerbank Battery: More and more powerful batteries are now available on the market, and at lower prices. These are extremely useful to keep your gadgets charged when you might not have access to electrical outlets.

Phone Gimbal: Both action cameras and mobile phones are becoming more and more capable of shooting stable footage, even when filming from a shaking bicycle. In the past I found a gimbal to be a useful solution for taking videos with my iPhone but recently I haven't felt the need to carry one.

Tripod: If you are serious about your filming there might be occasions when a compact, light tripod would be useful.

Selfie Stick: More on this later but it can be used as a tool to film your trip.

Torch: Most mobile phones now have this function available so it is for you to decide whether you need a separate torch. Should you spend a lot of time camping, a torch or even a head lamp could be useful to have at hand.

Odometer: Mobile phones can tell you how far you have traveled. However, to be accurate a mobile phone needs an app running in the background as you cycle. This is quite a drain on the battery if used all day and so I never use this option. I prefer to take a dedicated odometer attached to the bike to tell me at a glance how far I have traveled.

Bike Lights: It goes without saying that cycling in poor visibility, let alone at night, is not very sensible. During bad weather or when you have to get through a long tunnel, bike lights are essential. I always bring a detachable set of front and rear lights that I attach to the bike if I feel I need to. I also like lights that can be recharged using a USB cable. This way you don't need to worry if the batteries run out as you are able to recharge them every now and then. Detachable lights are cheap and easy to find and what I like about them is that they can also be hung on the roof inside your tent to provide you with enough lighting.

Solar Panel: These are also becoming more affordable and efficient in providing energy that you can store in your battery as you are cycling. Especially in sunny conditions, even a small solar panel sitting on one of your bags as you ride can give you enough energy to charge most of your gadgets during the night.

Lanyard: I use a lanyard as a way to secure my mobile phone. A lanyard around your neck or wrist is an effective way to prevent your phone dropping and breaking. As you will frequently use it during the day, often with sweaty hands or gloves, a lanyard attached to a good protective case is an insurance policy against any accident that might damage it. A less obvious advantage of using a lanyard when wearing it around your neck, is that it stabilises your shots when filming with a smartphone.

The Others Section is for some miscellaneous items which mostly concern camping equipment. If you are not considering camping at all, most things I mention in this section will not be necessary.

Tent: Carrying a tent with you, even if you don't intend to use it often, gives you the peace of mind to know that in an emergency, no matter where you are, you will be able to stop and be protected for the night. You will find more details on the most suitable types of tent to carry in the following chapter.

Mattress: Inflatable mattresses are becoming more affordable and popular. The most compact and light are rolled small enough to fit into one hand and once inflated can offer comfort and insulation while you camp at night. Foam mattresses that can be rolled up and tied to the bike are also popular for bike touring. They are extremely cheap and very light, but do have some disadvantages; they are bulky, not as comfortable to sleep on and harder to fit into a compact luggage set up. One possible solution which I have found in the past, is to use them as the outer layer protecting your bike package. A more wasteful option would be to purchase one when you arrive at your destination and dispose of it once your trip is over.

Pillow: In the past, in order to save some ounces, I used a compression bag with all my clean clothes inside as a pillow. On more recent tours I carried an inflatable pillow. It is very compact and light, and will help you get a better night's sleep without breaking the bank.

Sleeping bag: Unless you are camping in very warm conditions at night this is another item you will want to carry. Down sleeping bags are the lightest and most compact, while still keeping you warm. They can cost much more than synthetic ones and should they get wet they are not easy to dry without a tumble dryer. Sleeping bags are also designed in different ways. Some are in the classic mummy style that tapers down the legs and feet to keep you warmer, while others have more of a duvet rectangular shape that allows you more movement making them more comfortable but not as warm.

Silk Liner: Extremely light, rolled up it is the size of a closed fist. They can give you some more insulation adding one or two degrees temperature to your sleep. As they can be regularly washed and dry fast, I like them as a way to keep the inside of the sleeping bag clean.

Zip ties: A Jack of all trades, I never leave without a selection of zip ties in different lengths and thicknesses. They can be used when packing the bike, fixing the under saddle bar that I use as a way to carry my backpack (more on this later), but mostly they can be a great DIY fix for emergencies when things break and need to be secured.

Small Lock: I carry at least one small lock with a numerical combination. I mostly use it to secure the zipper of my bike bag after I have packed it and it can also be handy in certain accommodations where you might have access to a locker. These are small and easily cut though so they shouldn't be relied upon for safety but rather used as a deterrent.

Bungee Straps: Another very useful item to carry. My Brompton rear rack comes with two bungee straps already installed but I still bring a couple of spares as they can be used to secure things on the bike or to carry things in emergencies.

Compression Bags: I have a selection of different sizes and colours. The ones I use are also waterproof to a certain extent which helps on rainy days. I use them to keep everything I carry well organised and tidy in the bike bags. Once you get used to the sizes and their colours you know exactly where to find what you are looking for and they go some way towards ensuring that you do not leave anything behind.

Zip Lock Bags: I carry a good selection of plastic bags with zip locks. They are light and don't take up any space. As they can be tightly sealed, they are a good way to further protect your documents for example, but can also function as storage for food that you haven't finished or as a way to carry light rubbish with you until you find a suitable place to dispose of it.

First Aid Kit: It is a good idea to have at least a simple First Aid Kit pouch with alcohol to disinfect a wound if you fall, a selection of band aid plasters, sterile gauze dressings, tweezers to use for basic emergencies. I was once scolded, having shown on one of my YouTube videos that I packed it at the bottom of my backpack. A fair point was raised that in certain situations, in order to be useful, a First Aid Kit should be packed with easy access.

Bringing a tent

Later in the 'Planning' chapter, I will discuss the different types of accommodation available. Tents, however, deserve a separate section as I think they are the perfect match to a bike tour. Despite this, tents are by no means indispensable when bike touring so let me clarify what I mean by this. Even when you are planning to rely on hotel rooms, there are a few points worth considering. Unlike with more traditional trips, where you rely on public transport, booked accommodation and timetables, when cycling you cannot always be sure of reaching your planned destination. The actual route might be tougher than you envisaged, or you could not feel that great on a particular day; maybe, despite planning your route ahead, you couldn't possibly consider the strong tailwind helping you or the good quality of a road that allows you to ride faster than anticipated, therefore wanting to push on further. Either way, even if you might not use it that much, bringing along a tent makes your plans more flexible. A tent will also heighten the sense of adventure and excitement and let you experience the freedom and simplicity that come when we connect with nature.

Modern tents are made of light and durable materials and for a couple of extra kilograms of weight you can bring a tent, a sleeping bag and an inflatable mattress that can give you the peace of mind that comes from knowing that no matter where you are, you will have the option of spending the night well sheltered. The freedom that comes with this is remarkable. Even when you plan to stay in a hotel, with a tent you can decide that there is no need to reserve your room in advance as it is not a necessity anymore. You can also check a hotel room in advance and feel free to move on if you are not happy with the quality or the price that is offered.

As for the type of tent, I recommend purchasing a free-standing type of tent. These are designed in such a way that they can be set up without the need to fix pegs into the ground, therefore allowing you to pitch a tent pretty much anywhere. A free standing tent simply relies on tent poles to stay upright and can be used even on a slab of cement or tarmac. There might be times when you are not left with too many options and this versatility could become extremely useful.

A final consideration is whether to bring a single or a double tent. While I used to tour with a single tent, over the last few years I have moved to using a double tent. I feel that for the little extra weight they add you get much more comfort and, on a Brompton, even the ability to store your bike inside. This is something you will appreciate particularly on occasions when you are forced to spend more time in the tent than just the night; for example there will be times when you have to sit out some bad weather or you feel you need to get a little more rest.

A tent, like other technical equipment, will need some practice and testing. Time spent learning how to pitch it effectively will be invaluable once you start touring.

Cycling luggage setup

Once you have settled on your list of things to bring, now comes the time to decide how best to carry them on and off the bike. By thinking about both these aspects, you will have to find a setup that is flexible enough to work well on all steps of your journey. Some folding bikes have been designed specifically for touring and might have ready made solutions that include custom bags and attachments. If this is the case for you, you will not need to make too many changes in order to find something that works. On the other hand the majority of folding bikes do not fit into this category and will need a different approach, which can bring its own advantages.

When bike touring on any bike there are usually two different approaches. The more traditional one uses multiple pannier bags that attach to a front and a rear rack. The second approach is a more recent trend that is usually referred to as 'bikepacking'. It was born out of the fact that it is not always easy, or indeed possible, to fit racks to non-specific touring bikes. A light racing bike in aluminum or carbon, or even a mountain bike, might not have the necessary attachments to fit a rack and panniers; even if they do, their frames are usually not designed with a wheelbase long enough to give enough clearance and your heels might hit the bags while you pedal. To overcome these limitations and allow any bike to be used for touring, specific bags are now popular on the market; they use straps and custom shapes that allow them to be fitted unobtrusively on the frame of the bike itself, as well as under the saddle or around the handlebar. This setup has a reduced capacity when it comes to volume but is lighter and faster. Furthermore, with a mountain bike, it is the best solution to use on rough terrains where too much shaking and rattling could easily damage racks and panniers.

Most folding bikes won't allow you to go entirely either way. As mentioned earlier, the usual 16" or 20" wheels make panniers hard to use, while the small frame makes most bikepacking bags hard to fit. What is needed therefore is a little more creativity and a solution that is a bit of a mix of the two approaches.

To point you in the right direction, ask yourself three simple questions:

❖ Is this setup easy and safe to cycle with?

❖ Is it simple and fast to pack the bike ready to be transported?

❖ Can you walk carrying the folded bike and everything else as well?

Pretty much from the beginning of my touring on a folding bike, I have settled on a versatile setup that I think meets the above criteria while still allowing me to carry a good amount of luggage. I haven't invented anything original, but have hit on a solution that was discovered whilst doing some research on how others had been doing it before me. This was then slightly modified and adapted after some trial and error. Although it is something I use specifically on my bike model, I believe it can be tweaked and easily adapted to most folding bikes available on the market. What the right setup is for you also depends on the volume of your luggage and whether it is possible to fit specific bags on the bike you have. If you intend to use your folding bike for touring rather than commuting to work or for leisure cycling in a city, the ability to fit custom bags solutions to your model should be an important criteria for choosing the right one in the first place.

If your bike doesn't have the right fitting to clip a large bag at the front or to install a rear rack, not everything is lost. Some kind of bikepacking hacks will still be possible, for example by using a range of bags such as a saddle bag, and other frame bags that you can tie, usually by velcro straps, around the handlebar or frame of the bicycle. The main limitation of a bikepacking setup is reduced capacity. Despite new saddle bags on the market providing more and more space, they are still rather compact. This won't prevent you from touring, but choices of what you can and can't take with you will have to be made. A simple choice not to do any camping, for example, would reduce the bulk of your gear considerably.

A Brompton setup

The setup I use on a Brompton **(fig. 20)** includes two main bags. The larger capacity one is fixed at the rear of the bike and is a simple rucksack that you might also use for trekking or travelling and could well be something you already have. The one I tour with has 45 litres capacity and it fits everything I need. The bag fixed at the front of the bike is more specific. Most folding bikes come with the option to attach a mounting block at the front of the frame that is used to clip on an array of bags of different brands and capacity that are sold on the market. **(fig. 21)**

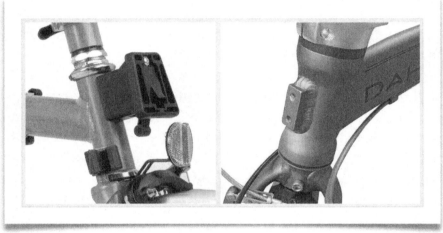

~ *(fig. 21)* ~

The bag I use has a roll on top and can store up to 30 litres and hold a weight of up to 10 kilograms.

It is good to consider leaving a little empty space in both bags for things that you might have to carry during the day. If right at the start both bags are completely stuffed full you won't have any space left to carry the food you bought for the evening or a spare bottle of water. Let me now describe in some detail both how these two are fitted on the bike and how I use them while cycling.

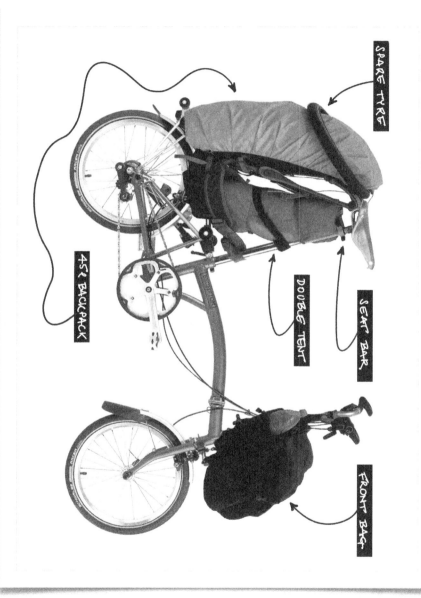

~ *(fig. 20)* ~

Front Bag:

This is the bag that contains everything I need to be able to access whilst cycling and is also where I store my passport, mobile phone and other valuables. **(fig. 22)** Clipped on the frame and just in front of the handlebar, it is very easy to access any time I need something. The one I own, as mentioned, is a 30 litre capacity bag which also has two external pouches facing the rider side. One has a secure zip and is perfect for carrying my wallet; also the mobile phone as well as the powerbank battery with its cable that I can connect to the solar panel when I need to. The other pocket is wide enough to fit a 1.5 litre water bottle which is easy to access whenever I am thirsty.

Moving to the main compartment, it has a roll top design that is fast to open by accessing two side buckles. For this reason I use it to store things that I frequently need during the day. Snacks and food I eat while riding go here; furthermore this is where I put my action camera and other equipment I use for filming, a sweater and a light rain jacket, a pair of warm gloves and a woollen hat, depending on the climate, as well as cables, batteries and plugs I need when recharging my gadgets. Last but not least, I also store a rain cover that I can quickly access should the weather turn stormy. The bag itself does have some waterproof qualities but, as it contains electronics and other expensive items, having a further rain cover to protect it ensures that everything inside is kept dry. There are a few reasons why it makes sense to store the most important items in this bag. First, as it is easily detached by unclipping it from the block it is attached to, it can be quickly removed and carried. I never leave this bag unattended and carry it with me each time I need to park the bike, let's say for a quick stop at a local store or to eat lunch at a restaurant. Secondly, while riding, it gives me peace of mind to see it in front of me at all times; this way I can be sure that it is fixed securely on the bike and that I haven't forgotten to close a compartment and run the risk that something might slip out. When I am stopping in a crowded location with people all around me, again being able to have it in front will ensure that nobody can easily access it.

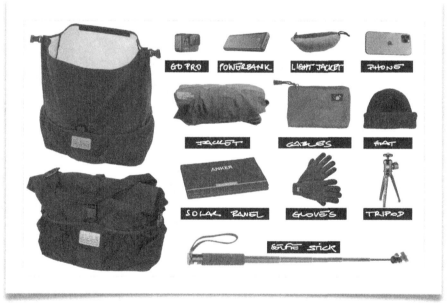

~ *(fig. 22)* ~

Rear Bag:

The rear of the bike is bearing most of your weight when cycling, putting a lot of strain on the rear wheel. Because of this I try to use the rear bag for all those things that I rarely use and everything that is bulky but light. **(fig. 23)**

~ (fig. 23) ~

At the bottom I usually fold flat the IKEA Dimpa bag and the soft bag that I use to transport the bike. If I know that I will take some public transport on that day, it makes sense to put it somewhere in easier reach. Next I normally pack some spare innertubes and the pouch with all the tools I need for emergency repairs. On top of that goes pretty much all the camping equipment with the exception of the tent that is tied around the seatpost. **(fig. 20)** Then I put the two compression sacks, with the clean clothes in one and clothes that need to be washed in the other. Next the pouch with all the toiletries, a towel and food I won't be eating during the day and that can be safely stored. Even this bag has a roll top closing system, which I prefer because it allows you to adjust to the varying bulk you may be carrying at any given time. A backpack in the range of 40 to 50 litres is usually plenty of capacity. A backpack with some sort of metal plate or rigid frame on its back is the ideal as it makes it much more stable on the bike and will avoid some sagging. Find something as light as possible yet sturdy, paying special attention to the shoulder straps; these should be resistant, not easily frayed and with an adjustable length that doesn't easily slide. It sounds complicated, but in reality most reputable brands in outdoor stores offer trekking rucksacks that will meet all requirements.

To securely fix a regular rucksack, provided your folding bike has a rear rack installed, all that you will need is a bar, a few thick, large sized zip ties or a couple of leather straps and 2 bungee cords. **(fig. 24)**

~ *(fig. 24)* ~

The bar could be a metal tube, a thick wooden pole or a fancy carbon fibre tube if you want it to be light! Care should be taken to choose something that won't easily snap or break. For a decade, I have successfully used a hollow metal tube which was originally one leg of a microphone stand. Chances are that you will have already something around that you can use for this task. As it will hold the shoulder straps of the rucksack its width should be roughly the width of your shoulders or about 40 cm.

Use your large zip ties or a couple of leather straps to fix the bar horizontally just below the saddle. The easiest way to do so is to loop two ties or straps around each end of the bar a couple of times, before threading them to the metal frame parts under the saddle. In order for the bar to work as expected, it should be tight and well leveled horizontally without any slant on either side. It is a good idea to use another set of thinner zip ties, one on each side, to function as a backup in case the large one fails, something which has never happened to me. Once this bar is fixed, the shoulder harnesses are simply looped around each side holding the rucksack upright.

Trekking rucksacks usually come with a waistband. I use this to further secure the bag by clipping it around the bike seatpost. **(fig. 20)**

What remains now is to fix the bottom part of the rucksack to the rack of the bike. This is necessary for two reasons: first, to further secure the bag on the bike and make it more stable;

but also to pull its lower part away from your heels, which might otherwise touch it as you pedal.

Lean the bottom of the rucksack on the rear rack platform by adjusting the length of the leather straps evenly either side. Next fix the rucksack firmly with a couple of bungee cords looped around it and inside the harnesses. You do so by attaching the hooks on the cords to the frame of the rack. An even better way, which is what I use, is to put a carbon fibre tube horizontally inside the lower straps and loop the bungee cords around both sides. **(fig. 25)** This will achieve the same aim of pulling the bag towards the rear of the bike but will also add more balance.

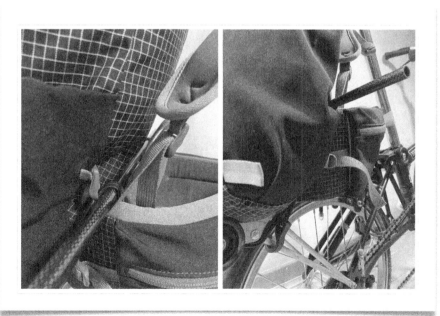

~ (fig. 25) ~

To conclude, I think this setup is extremely flexible, not only while riding the bike but also when you need to take a taxi from the airport, a train or a bus to the starting point of your journey. All you have to do is fold the bike, put the tent inside the front bag and the rucksack on your shoulders and you are able to move freely onto a train platform or ready to queue at the taxi stand.

Using Trailers

You might rightly point out that I have ignored another tried and tested way of loading a bicycle with luggage: trailers. They are indeed another effective way to carry stuff on a bike while touring, with many cyclists swearing by them. I must admit to not having any experience using them, but there is one main reason why I think they are not ideal with a folding bike.

I have already talked about the main advantage folding bikes can bring to cycle touring, namely their portability. A trailer would cancel out that ease of traveling almost completely; despite having your compact bike, needing to deal with a metal frame, one or two more wheels and a large platform is cumbersome and would make it so much harder to move around when not cycling. While a trailer might be a good idea if you are starting and finishing your cycling tour right outside your front door, for any other kind of tour you will likely end up trading the ease of being able to conveniently transport your bike. Storing it in a small bag and jumping on a bus or putting it in a car boot when you need a lift, will no longer be a convenient options.

I cannot tell from experience how pulling a trailer might affect the ride, but another concern I would have is the fact that it has the potential to add further complications and parts that could break. You will possibly need extra tyres and tools in order to repair it, and should something go wrong while riding, you will find it really hard if not impossible to carry on with your journey. Panniers and racks can also be vulnerable at times, but your luggage is more evenly spread out and you will likely find a way to tie a broken bag to the bike or patch up a damaged rack without letting it spoil the rest of your trip.

~ Part II ~

Planning

Choosing a destination

The most exciting part of planning must be sitting down and pondering where to travel to next. Sifting through wishes, expectations and affordability, we narrow down the choices to a shortlist of places that we expect to be interesting and fascinating. The same process applies when deciding to go on a bicycle tour, only further complemented by a few extra considerations. What makes for a good cycling destination will also depend, at least to a certain extent, on your physical fitness, experience, the amount of time available, the weather conditions and season in which you will be traveling, and the quality of roads or cycleways, as well as safety concerns.

Physical fitness has already been discussed in a previous section. The message I wanted to convey was that bike touring should not be limited to young and sporty athletes. However, this does not mean that one should not be aware of one's own limits. Doing so could lead to unnecessary disappointment and, in the worst cases, could also be dangerous. This is particularly true for those who do not have any previous experience with bike touring and might therefore not be able to differentiate what is feasible from what is hard or impossible. Like with any activity, what works best is to take small steps first, which will build your strength and confidence and allow you to push further and challenge yourself. Your body will react very differently, depending on whether you are riding a roller coaster road in the mountains or following the Rhine river on a smooth cycleway as flat as a pancake. In this sense an honest assessment of your level of fitness should be considered when choosing a destination.

As with any independent form of travel, a bike tour will test you much more than an all inclusive package holiday where everything is taken care of for you. Previous experience will make a whole lot of difference to how you deal with things. Books and manuals like the one you are reading can help you to be better prepared and will save you some time, but ultimately real learning comes from practice. Different places will challenge you in different ways. This is indeed one of the reasons why traveling is so appealing. While some parts of the world will be very familiar, others will feel completely alien and you will have to be more resourceful. What works and what doesn't work for you can only be learnt by experiencing it.

A bike tour is bound to be slower than what you are used to. While the highlights of some countries can be visited in a matter of days by using planes, cars, trains and buses, on a bicycle it is likely that it will take quite a bit longer. I have highlighted the advantages of a folding bike in reducing this gap, but still most of the distance you cover will be done by cycling, otherwise there wouldn't be much point in carrying one along with you. Depending on the distances involved and the time you have available, one location could be more suitable than another.

Climate affects cycling more than some other activities because you are exposed to the elements day after day. No amount of careful planning will help you avoid the occasional downpour, but extreme conditions can make any cycling uncomfortable; a little research into what kind of weather you may encounter in a place and when is the best season to travel should inform your choices. Wind can also be a challenge in certain places and when you are planning your route you might find ways to use prevailing wind patterns to your advantage. Similarly, visiting a tropical country in the midst of a rainy season is something you might tolerate when traveling in luxury but should probably be avoided when cycling. Humidity and temperatures can also make things much more challenging. Sadly, in a few parts of the world, air pollution can also be a problem, especially when spending many hours exercising in the open.

As for the quality of road networks and availability of cycleways, countries come in all flavours. In the Netherlands you could cycle for months on bicycle lanes without worrying about traffic, while in developing countries, if you want tarmac, you will most likely have to follow the main highway. Your preferences will again play a part in deciding which place best meets your expectations and conforms to the boundaries you have set. Similarly the quality of the road surfaces will affect the type of cycling. In certain areas it might be possible to stick to tarmac while in others there may be nothing more than trails and rough roads that are not ideal for a folding bicycle. Whether riding solo or as part of a group you will need different levels of self-sufficiency according to how remote or densely populated a destination is. This will influence the equipment you carry, and the list that was discussed earlier might need to be tweaked accordingly.

Safety concerns are of course something we should always consider when deciding on the next destination for our holiday. Later, I will dedicate an entire section to dispelling one of the most common misconceptions about bike touring: namely, that it is dangerous. It really isn't and if you still have some doubts I hope I will be able to convince you. Having said that, a cyclist could be more vulnerable in places where safety is an issue. These are few and far between, but there are places where tourism without some kind of support from travel agents and local guides could be risky and ill advised, especially for a foreigner traveling on his own. If you have any doubts as to the safety of your destination, do some research in advance. A good place to start is your national embassy or foreign office advice regarding specific countries. Unfortunately, different nationalities can on rare occasions have an impact on your safety while traveling. However, when reading official advice do bear in mind that it is very cautious by nature. Compare it with recent information you might be able to source online from other cyclists' blogs or websites. I did tour in countries which were deemed unsafe for an independent traveler; surprisingly they turned out to be some of the most hospitable places I have had the luck to visit.

How much will it cost

You will be pleased to know that cycle touring can be one of the cheapest options when it comes to traveling. You are independent in transportation, and if you are willing to use a tent every now and then, even accommodation costs can be manageable and adapted to what you are comfortable spending. I am aware that it is impossible to provide an accurate figure; all that matters here, is the ability to give a fair assessment of the kind of travel that will be affordable. As we are budgeting for a specific holiday, costs incurred in buying the bicycle and other equipment you might need will not be included in the exercise. These are fixed costs, investments you make over time and that hopefully will be used on several trips.

Many variables will affect costs. Some of them are obvious and barely worth mentioning, but I will do so for the sake of clarity. They answer questions beginning with 'where', 'how', 'when' and 'what'. Where you will be traveling to and how long for, are maybe two of the main items affecting the final expenditure. Whether your bike tour requires a long haul flight ticket to get you to the starting point or you are able to start right outside your front door, will have quite an impact on the bottom line too. Traveling with others will work out to be cheaper - you can share the costs of hotel rooms, whose fees would probably be the same even if you were on your own, as hotels mostly charge prices per room rather than per person.

Next comes food, which shouldn't be skimped on as it is fuel for cyclists! Whether you are cooking all or some of your meals while camping, eating at food stalls, buying cold food in grocery stores or splashing out on fine dining, will of course affect the cost considerably. The time of travel will also matter. Prices during peak season as opposed to off-peak time could turn out to be very different indeed.

In trying to get an idea of what can be afforded, a good place to start is to set a maximum budget you are willing to allocate for the tour. Next begin by removing all the unavoidable costs that can be determined even before departure. When transportation is necessary, begin to include the cost of air, train or ferry tickets. If using an airline, the good news is that a small folding bike should help you trim some of the further charges that are often levied when carrying bicycles or general sports equipment. If you are required to obtain a visa for entry into a country its fee should also be included in the tally, as should the costs of vaccinations when needed or travel insurance should you opt for this. Conveniently these are all costs that can be accurately estimated even before committing to the final purchase. All that is needed is a quick search online. This is as far as science can go, what comes next is more akin to fortune telling, but is well worth pondering.

What needs to be considered now are the costs incurred during the journey which are by nature variable; however, these can be controlled, to a certain extent, according to the way you decide to travel. Having added up all predictable costs, subtract them from the total amount of your budget and divide the result by the number of days you are planning for your holiday in order to obtain a daily budget. Whether you are planning to stay in hotel rooms and eat out in restaurants most times, or are comfortable camping and eating on a budget, will make a lot of difference and give you some room for manoeuvre. The figure you arrive at will not be 100% precise but will be very useful; it will allow you to assess if your daily budget is sufficient to meet the comfort level you are looking for in the particular place you have chosen as a destination. If you have more than one place in mind, one way to decide which will work best is to repeat the same exercise for each one of them.

If your budget cannot be stretched and the trip does not look as affordable as first thought, there are a few things that can be done to help reduce costs. The most obvious one is to give up some comfort. Having a tent with you will reduce accommodation costs. You could stay on a campsite, since these are usually about half the price of a budget hotel room, but you could also decide to 'wild camp' a few nights or most nights, something which will not cost you anything. I will talk in detail about wild camping in a separate section. Similarly with food, cooking your own food, if you bring a stove, or putting up with daily groceries and cold food you can source from supermarkets, will make a difference on your overall budget. It is no surprise that on a bike tour, accommodation and food costs will account for most of the total expenses. When on a tight budget another option worth mentioning is to take advantage of the hospitality of fellow cyclists. At the time of writing 'warmshowers.org' has been for many years a free popular online tool for cyclists. There you will be able to get in touch with hosts who welcome cyclists into their homes for a night. Of course what is offered will vary from a nice spare bedroom, to a couch or at times space for your tent in their garden. Both hosts and guests are active on these platforms, and usually will reply to your messages with a few days notice. The best thing about such an option is the fact that pretty much all of the hosts are bike touring enthusiasts and will be able to offer great tips and suggest the best roads for riding in any given area. It is of course also a rare opportunity while travelling to experience life as it is lived by the locals. Some savings can also be made by avoiding peak season, especially in popular destinations. Travel off peak if at all possible according to the weather; it will work out much cheaper but also roads will be much quieter and you will be able to ride without excessive noise and traffic.

Route planning

Before delving into route planning it has to be said that for some people it is unnecessary. The argument goes that any planning will somehow diminish the freedom of travel, removing the unknowns that come with an adventure, those mishaps and chance encounters that can make it even more memorable. Those who on the other hand think it is necessary will argue that it better prepares you for the unexpected and sets manageable rides that can help you reach your destination, while the research involved better informs you and as a consequence keeps you safer. An aspect worth considering is the fact that for most people a touring holiday involves at least precise dates for the departure and the return, and the ability to meet these deadlines when cycling depends in part on some sort of structure and advance planning. Ultimately each person's character will decide whether they need a plan at all. If you are in the 'plan-less' group feel free to skip this section.

I do like to keep organised, so the need for route planning comes naturally. I don't see it as a chore but as time well spent and enjoyable, which makes me look forward to the trip even more. In the 'route planners' camp there are two separate trends. Some are still attached to past analog times and love the feeling of holding paper maps in their hands, while others embrace the plethora of digital assistance that is now available. For convenience and ease of use I find that the internet has transformed the way we can plan by providing real time data at our fingertips that is impossible to match. If you still like your traditional maps, nothing prevents you using them as an additional resource or while you are actually on the tour. You can tailor your route plan to be more or less detailed according to your preferences. It can vary from a meticulous breakdown of your trip day by day to a looser framework that gives you a little structure while still allowing you to modify and adapt to what emerges during your ride.

General Plan

One way to start planning effectively is to make good use of one of the many satellite mapping tools available on the internet. Once your location has been chosen and you are clear about the places and roads you want to visit and ride, begin to plot on the map a series of points and link them into a tentative route. The purpose of this first iteration is to simply give an idea of the distance involved between your starting point and your final destination. Chances are that this distance will be a conservative estimate only; once you delve deeper into your daily routes you will find diversions, smaller roads or cycleways that might be more pleasant to ride and will always add mileage when compared to the main road. To compensate for this discrepancy always err on the cautious side. As an example, you could add an arbitrary percentage increase of 20% to the distance you first obtained. Depending on the destination chosen, the season you are traveling in could also make a big difference, with longer or shorter daylight hours available for cycling.

Once you have the approximate distance involved, you next need to define the number of days you are able to spend cycling. If your tour involves transportation to get you to the starting point and to return home, these should be accounted for. Do check approximate times of arrival and departure available and consider the need to adapt to other variables such as jet lag that might be involved in a long haul flight as opposed to a journey where you do not change time zones. An early morning arrival could give you the chance to put in your first day's ride, while arriving in the afternoon or evening will not allow you to do that much. When time is limited you will want to make the most of each day, but do bear in mind that travel is tiring and if at all possible it is a good idea to acclimatise first and have some good rest before setting off on your journey. Similarly, when the time comes to return take timetables into consideration. An early morning flight, for example, would mean that you should spend the night before within easy reach of the airport. On the other hand, should your flight depart in the evening or at night-time, it would give you half a day or even a full day to put in your final ride, reaching the airport by bike if at all possible. Building a little slack into your schedule at this point is also sensible advice. I would normally add a day or two every ten days or so as a way to ensure that I am able to complete my planned route in good time. There may be times on a bicycle when you will want to do less than you planned or stay longer in a place you like. Having a few days to play with will give you the opportunity to be a little more flexible with your choices and better prepared for all eventualities.

The mileage you have calculated can then be divided by the number of days you are able to ride, resulting in the approximate daily average mileage that will be required. Now some consideration should be given as to whether this mileage is manageable. Whether it is or not will depend on the types of road, your experience, your level of fitness and whether you are willing to challenge yourself or are looking for a more relaxed and enjoyable ride. For those who have previously done some touring, chances are you already know what a comfortable daily average distance might be. For those that haven't, without trying to be scientific about it, I can offer an approximation to start with. As a rule of thumb, on a good surfaced road with a few hill climbs but no extreme conditions, I would suggest three different distances associated with the level of effort needed to cover them.

According to how challenging you want your tour to be, I recommend starting with 60 km per day for a leisurely cycling holiday, 80km for one of moderate difficulty and anything above 100km for something more demanding. When I tour on my folding bike I find that 80km hits the sweet spot and is the daily distance that I find most comfortable. If you are new to bike touring this might seem hard, but it is actually quite feasible. On a cycling holiday you spend a good part of the day riding the bicycle: averaging 15 kilometres per hour, which is not too hard to achieve, it will take you 5 hours and 20 minutes, while if you aim for an easier 60km per day it will take about 4 hours of cycling. When deciding on a particular distance, there is one more aspect to bear in mind. One of the joys of traveling is to visit interesting sites, appreciate the local food and culture, and at times relax in the sun. Some of it will be experienced while cycling, but you should also include enough breaks to stop and enjoy some leisure time.

If in doubt as to what is going to feel more comfortable for you, the best way to figure it out is to go on a few test rides where you cover those distances and see how it goes. If you are doing these test rides without any weight on the bike, consider that it will be a bit harder when you are carrying a few bags. On the other hand, also take into account that when touring, your body will get fitter day by day and what felt arduous at first might feel much easier by the end of your trip. This is also the time when I start filling in the 'Route Planner' and in particular the 'Calendar' sheet. It is simply a list that displays the outline of my journey and gives, at a glance, the general details of what I will be doing each day.

What can one do if there isn't enough time to cover the planned route? This is when a folding bike can come in handy! If there is an option and you don't mind doing so, simply find out whether a not so interesting section can be skipped by taking a bus transfer or a train journey.

Specific Plan

If you feel the need to be more detailed in your planning you can now break it down into specific stages that you will more or less follow day by day. If you are willing to give it the time, this can be a useful exercise as it will allow you to fine tune things. Whilst the 'general plan', just outlined, gave us a good idea of the feasibility of a tour within a certain timeframe, the 'specific plan' will refine it and make it possible to complete the tour in the most efficient way.

A simple example will make this clear. Dividing a 1000 kilometres journey into ten 100 kilometres stages will not prove to be very useful. Despite having assigned the same generic distance to cover, the effort needed to do so will always be different and there will not be two days that feel exactly the same. In exceptional circumstances, when you know that you will be cycling on completely flat terrain from the beginning to the end of your journey, this approach might work, but otherwise it is quite unrealistic. Even in such circumstances you will have to consider the availability of accommodation or camping sites available on the way, which means that some days you will have to stop short of your planned mileage while other times you will have to pedal further.

By delving in more detail into each stage you can consider the kind of roads you will ride on a particular day, paying attention to things such as the grade profile of an uphill climb or the total elevation gain. Clearly, knowing that on a particular day you will have to climb from sea level to a mountain pass above 2000 metres of altitude, while the following day will start with a descent from the top back to the sea, will allow you to adapt the distance you are going to ride to this difference in difficulty. You could for example allocate

70 kilometres for the uphill stage whilst deciding that 130 kilometres over a long descent will not be that uncomfortable to complete. Other similar considerations should be taken into account. The quality of the roads could be excellent one day but very poor on another. There might be days when there are a lot of interesting sites to visit while others that will not involve stops for sightseeing; this will of course affect the distance you are able to cover. It is not an exact science, but in certain locations prevailing winds directions can be predicted quite accurately, and whether you are cycling in one direction or another could make a world of difference to the effort that is required. Earlier, I mentioned how I find that 80 kilometres a day is a good distance to aim for. Despite this, when planning my route on the Carretera Austral in Patagonia, I knew that riding on a rocky road rather than on tarmac meant that such a distance would be too ambitious; I aimed for daily rides that ranged from 40 kilometres to a maximum 60 per day. Similarly, I was much more cautious when planning my Ladakh trip, since there one is often riding above 4000 metres of altitude.

Using a satellite map on your phone, computer or tablet, you can magnify and work out the roads you will follow in more detail. Another excellent way to find out which are the best roads to follow in any given place is by reading accounts on other cyclists' blogs. For some it might seem   like spoiling some of that surprise that is part of any adventure, but it can often help you make informed choices between following a route that is full of traffic or boring and one that is much more scenic and ideal for riding a bicycle. Online maps, as well as many other mapping tools and phone apps, will allow you to see the daily profile of the road with the hills and peaks that need climbing and help you gauge how hard or easy each day is going to be. Many of these tools are also especially focused towards cycling and will highlight the best routes to follow on a bicycle.

When looking at the route in this level of detail you could choose the points of interest to stop at for a visit, and any diversions you might want to make to do so. It can also be a good idea to take notes about places where water and food are available and where you will find accommodation. Highlight those sections where food supplies or even water will be hard to come by and jot down a reminder on the previous day to stock up whatever is necessary for the following day. This can be invaluable if you are touring remote places where distances between towns and villages can sometimes span several days, and it can make a world of difference whether you were prepared or not.

It is good practice in route planning to bear in mind that no matter how fit you are at the start, chances are that you will build up more strength and stamina with each passing day. Make the first few days a little easier to allow for this adaptation; the middle part of your journey is when you will be at your strongest, while at the end, especially if you haven't given yourself regular rest days, you might start feeling more tired.

Now I transfer all this information into the 'Route Planner' by filling in a separate 'Day' sheet for each stage of cycling, including a daily map with altimetry and all the detailed information such as distances between towns or services, places to stop for sightseeing as well as hotels or campsites where I could spend the night. Finally, and particularly important if you are travelling on your own, do share your route with at least a member of your family or a friend. This will be reassuring for them, as they will be able to trace your route, but also for you; you will travel with the peace of mind that comes from knowing that those close to you are aware of your whereabouts on a daily basis and will be able to offer help if necessary.

Booking Accommodation

The decision to book accommodation in advance is a personal one and will affect the way you travel. Having fixed reservations along your entire route will be, for many, somehow reassuring. Knowing where you will be spending the night at any given point along your journey will take some time to research and book and probably cost a little more money, but it will save time during your travel. You will have the peace of mind that comes from not having to worry whether a room will be available and, having an address, you will know in advance how to reach it. This strategy can be particularly useful on trips that take you into popular locations, which in peak season are sought after by tourists. Having cycled all day, spending the evening looking for a room in such places can be frustrating, expensive and time consuming.

Wherever you are going, I think it makes a lot of sense to book accommodation at least for your arrival and departure days. If you are using some transportation to reach your starting point and again at the end of it, you will know well in advance your arrival and departure times. Navigating in and out of large city airports or stations on a bicycle is to be done cautiously; the tiredness accumulated from flying, maybe compounded by jet lag, will not be as conducive to a good day's cycling. Also remember that the bike will need assembling and the luggage sorting. In the unlucky event that something was damaged during transport, should you need it, a bike shop is easier to find in a city than in the countryside. Unless you arrive early morning and have plenty of time to take it gently, allow yourself a day or two for sightseeing, adjusting to a new climate, different food and a foreign currency; this will ensure you are well rested and able to enjoy the start of your cycling more. Similarly pay attention to your schedule on the last day before your return journey. A morning departure will likely mean arriving a day earlier, in order to ensure that you do not miss your train or flight and to allow enough time to sort your luggage and pack the bike, if necessary.

Advance bookings bring some negative aspects to be considered too. It has been mentioned before how covering distances on a bicycle can at times be less predictable than using regular transport. Were you to be slowed down by tiredness or bad weather, or tested by a technical issue with the bike, or even a puncture, you will somehow still have to stick to the original plan as much as possible. Cancelling a reservation on the same day will surely incur a one night charge that is not refundable. Moreover you might find yourself unable to reach your goal for that day, stuck somewhere with no alternative accommodation. With the exception of peak season tourist destinations, booking in advance comes at a premium; you will likely pay a higher price than you would by searching a room locally on the day you reach your place. If there is a decent availability of rooms, you can shop around, looking at a few of them before choosing the best deal. In some cases booking in advance with an online reservation or a travel agent, will turn out to be not exactly what you expected. Sometimes, the beautiful brochures with elegant rooms with balcony and sea view might not reflect reality. If you can check a room in person, before deciding to reserve it, you will be in a better position to assess whether it is really worth its price. Another slight disadvantage is that at any given point you might pass through a place that you really like, wishing you had the freedom to stay for the night but not being able to.

Depending on where you are going, it might be the case that there are plenty of options as far as accommodation is concerned. If you are touring in places with lots of hotels, bed and breakfast, hostels or family stays, it might be easy to never book anything in advance yet never have any problem finding something suitable when you want to call it a day. This removes the disadvantages of the previous option while maintaining a similar level of comfort, as well as much more freedom in adapting the planned route, at least to a certain extent.

If you are bike touring in more remote areas where any tourism infrastructure is absent or very basic, you will need to introduce a level of independence that only a tent or similar camping equipment can bring. It goes without saying that for these situations no advance booking is possible, so you have no choice. I have touched upon it earlier in the section about whether or not to bring a tent. I won't repeat myself, but I find that whether you are touring in an area with lots of accommodation options or in a remote location with none, a tent allows the ultimate freedom which is one of the joys of cycling. Personally, I always carry one. I brought one along on journeys where I knew I would need it most times as well as in other places where I wasn't so sure and ended up hardly using it; even in the latter, a couple of kilograms extra weight were well worth carrying for the peace of mind it brought, knowing that there would always be a shelter to rest in at night. Generally carrying a tent means that the only accommodation I book in advance is mostly limited to arrival and departure days.

Managing Money

During a bike tour managing money is not unlike managing money during any other kind of travel. It can be straightforward in places with good infrastructures for tourists, while a little challenging in others where facilities are sparse. These differences will determine how much you should rely on atm machines and use debit or credit cards, or whether you should carry cash as your best option. A little research into the country you are about to visit will likely clarify which is the most sensible approach. For most places a good approach is to diversify and have a good balance of both.

While more and more payments around the world are now possible digitally or using cards, in some countries cash still reigns, especially in rural areas or for those small daily purchases of groceries and food.

On my tours I have relied on three main options:

- ❖ A credit or debit card linked to funds in my bank account, one that I know I will be able to use abroad.

- ❖ A prepaid 'travel card', also sometimes referred to as 'currency cards'.

- ❖ Cash

Having different forms of payment available doesn't only allow you to be flexible in the way you pay but is also a good suggestion to prevent the risk of being completely stuck should you lose any of them or in the unlikely event of theft. For this to be effective though one has to store each one of them in a different location. Putting all your cards and all your cash into the same wallet is not a good idea, as losing it would prevent you from using any of them. Rather store each card in different bags if at all possible as a way to mitigate such a prospect. Include carrying a form of payment on your person, possibly concealed in a safe pocket of a garment you are wearing. I like to use a money belt as a way to store a little cash, usually in my own currency as it is going to be used only in case of emergency. These are belts that are waterproof to a certain extent and have a hidden zipper running along their length. This can be opened, and folded banknotes can be slid inside on the inside of the belt itself and function as a backup. I would normally bring that money back home unused, avoiding exchange rates that on cash transactions are often costly.

Debit or credit cards can be used for the larger expenses; they are widely accepted and ideal when you are settling bills for night stays in hotels or reservations of travel tickets or for sightseeing that you haven not booked in advance. Make sure that you keep a digital record of the phone number (usually provided at the back of the card) to call in case of loss or theft of the card itself. This can become useful should you need assistance from your bank when your card is declined, but more importantly to notify them and have them block the card when necessary. As a further back up, I take photos of the back and front of the cards I am carrying, and I usually save these in an email or on the cloud. Doing so will make it easy when you communicate with your bank as you can access information such as your bank account number, sort-code, expiry date, etc. I have already introduced the idea of a decoy wallet. Do not throw away or cut up your expired cards anymore! Use them for this purpose.

Prepaid Travel Cards have become very popular in recent years. These are provided by private companies that offer credit cards that can be loaded with different currencies that can then be used for payment abroad as well as for withdrawing local currency from ATM machines. The advantage they have over standard credit or debit cards is the fact that they usually offer very competitive exchange rates and will often help avoid the hidden charges of using an ATM machine in a foreign country. Unlike your main cards that are usually linked to your bank account, these can be loaded with money as needed by using an app on a mobile phone or logging into a site on the internet. Applying for one is normally quite straightforward and they don't charge any operational fees. As they are pre-loaded with funds they also allow for a tight control on what you are spending.

As far as cash is concerned, even for those places where it is essential to have it, it is probably not a good idea to cycle around with the full amount to cover the rest of your holiday. Unless impractical, such as in a remote stretch of land lasting for many days, it makes sense to carry only a few days worth of spending money, regularly withdrawing smaller quantities each time you have access to services in towns, villages or at petrol stations. In some regions, particularly in developing countries, main international currencies such as Euros or US dollars are useful to have and are accepted as if they were local currency. They will often be accepted at a very good exchange rate from locals eager to mitigate the effects of currency inflation. If you are using cash it is even more important to learn the value of the local currency and become familiar with how much each different banknote is worth and looks like.

Miscellaneous

It is hard to include all possible costs involved in planning a journey but I will now talk about some of the most common ones that often people consider when travelling.

Travel Insurance

Taking out travel insurance to cover expenses in the event of an accident during your holiday is usually standard advice recommended by travel agencies or when you book a trip online. The argument goes that the peace of mind it gives you is well worth the expense. A standard travel insurance will normally cover costs such as: trip cancellation, interruption or delays, baggage delays or loss, emergency medical expenses, evacuation to the nearest hospital and even repatriation to your country should this become necessary. In some instances your credit card might already provide some basic cover, so it is well worth checking this out in advance.

There is a caveat when bike touring which makes things a little more complicated and therefore expensive. Using a bicycle as the main means of transport on a holiday makes it fall into the 'adventure sport' category of most insurers, and as a result it will not be covered by a standard travel insurance. Adventure sports are normally considered as add-ons that you select from a list of activities, and this will raise the cost of the policy significantly. For bike touring it is even more important to read all the small print and disclaimers that are usually well hidden and far too easy to ignore. As an example, you might have some pre-existing medical conditions that will mean you are not covered for the activity you have chosen, turning your expensive insurance into a complete waste of money and time.

If money is not an issue, it would be a no-brainer and I would always recommend taking out insurance when cycle touring. For the rest of us however, with all necessary disclaimers, I will also offer a personal perspective and provide a few counter-arguments to enable you to make your own decision.

Of course insurance is all about risk, and deciding not to spend money on insurance means you are willing to take some. There are a few things to bear in mind. The greatest costs, should you be involved in an emergency or an accident, are the medical costs of being treated in a hospital. A worse case scenario and one that statistically is very unlikely to happen, is to have the sort of accident that needs long term treatment in an intensive care unit. Costs in these situations spiral up very quickly no matter where you are in the world; to be insured at such a time, despite the unhappy circumstances, is a bit like winning the lottery. These are the extremely rare situations that make it worth it and that, at least in part, you are paying for when you take out your policy. Moving down the scale are those accidents that are not as dire but might still require some treatment and maybe a few days or a week at the hospital. Again, statistically speaking, with a bit of care these are also extremely unlikely to happen and depending on where you are planning to go, they can be more or less manageable. This last point is the one to consider.

Costs of emergency treatment in a hospital in a developing country as opposed to the costs for the same treatment in a US private clinic are literally a world apart. In the former, costs for those lucky enough to be earning Euros or Dollars could be quite manageable, while the latter could quickly get you bankrupt. I have taken several trips in the US, and on all but one occasion I made sure that I traveled with proper insurance; the one I left out, was a risk which paid off in the end but saw me cycling with extreme caution and attention at all times! The same is true of evacuation costs that could be necessary in a rescue from a remote location; they will also vary accordingly. While a helicopter rescue in Pakistan could be affordable, it would likely cost you very dearly in Europe or in the United States or in Australia. In case of an accident that needs treatment but does not put your life at risk, at least immediately, repatriation is always the best course of action. If you have decided to not take out insurance you must be sure to have at your disposal the funds necessary for an emergency flight ticket, which could be more expensive than your original ticket

For most other incidents, still rare but statistically more likely to happen, you would probably cope with what you have saved from not taking out insurance in the first place. No matter where you are, a medication prescription or a quick visit to a doctor should not be outrageously expensive; and it should give you enough help to then decide if you can continue or should rather return home to get some treatment. The rest of what an insurance covers, ranges from small annoyances to things that could spoil a trip, but will not lead to financial ruin.

Nothing is risk free in life, whether we are playing this wonderful game and taking part in it or trying to live in a cocoon of perceived safety. Nobody should take risks recklessly, but there are times when an informed risk is a risk well taken. It is beyond the scope of this manual to talk about long term travel or extreme expeditions, suffice to say that if all of them had required mandatory insurance, many would never have been undertaken. Many individuals have toured around the world on their bikes without insurance and have done so not out of stupidity or bravery; taking out insurance to cover such extended travels that may span dozens of countries is not always an option; and even if it is, the expense might force a hard choice, to either go for it anyway or to stop dreaming.

Passport Visas

As part of your planning you might want to look at your passport expiry date carefully and check the passport expiration rules of the country you are heading to. It goes without saying that travelling internationally on a soon-to-expire passport can put your entire trip in jeopardy. There is more to passport expiry than the date indicated on the passport. Every country will have its own passport expiration rules and different entry requirements. A good rule to follow is to ensure that it is valid six months past your travel date. The reason for this is that many countries will let you stay without a visa for up to six months. Depending on where you live and your situation a renewal application can take some time to be processed and you wouldn't want any delay to mess up your carefully drawn plans.

Visas are another necessity in some countries and getting one can at times be a cumbersome process. Give yourself enough time to research whether you need one in the first place and to figure out what documents need to be prepared and where they should be submitted. How easy or hard it is to get a visa depends on your nationality, the ability to pay for a fast track service, the political situation in your destination country and all the (often changing) unwritten rules.

Some countries make the process easier by allowing a visa to be issued once you arrive at the gate of entry of an international airport, while others will need to be completed in your home country and demand a lengthy list of documents. Another issue that visas can pose is the fact that some countries issue them with an expiry date they need to be used by. This of course doesn't allow for planning far in advance. Of course the internet will be your best friend: look up the official websites of the countries you want to visit and read their current regulations.

Be aware of the fact that there are countries where governments like to have control not only over their citizens but also over visiting tourists. When this is the case, even if it is not illegal, they will not encourage riding a bicycle and staying wherever your moods might take you! If this is the case the best strategy when applying for a visa is not to mention bike touring as a main purpose of your trip; doing so might mean that it gets rejected. Some places in order to issue a permit will want to have a detailed itinerary and proof of reservations where you will be spending each night over your entire stay. This again is hardly practical when cycling and the only way around it is to make bookings online that you are able to cancel at a later date: a little unethical, but it is the only way to ensure that your request will be granted. If one is necessary, don't forget to include its costs. Visa fees and associated costs range from 20 euros or dollars to over 100 for some countries.

Vaccination

Another necessary precaution when travelling the world, is to protect yourself from potentially serious illnesses. Parts of the world, including Africa, South East Asia, South America, and even Europe, can pose a health risk for tourists. Travel vaccinations can provide protection against a wide range of diseases. Which vaccines you need, if any, will of course depend on the destination. For other illnesses, vaccines are not available and other preventive measures should be taken. To ensure you are taking all necessary precautions, speak to your health provider and ask whether any vaccinations are mandatory in the area you are visiting. In some cases, not being vaccinated and having a certificate to prove it will prevent you entering the country.

Touring

Overcoming fears

Finally, after a lengthy discussion on bikes, equipment and planning, the time has come. The departure date is drawing closer and what was at first only an idea will start to feel more real; you will likely be very excited, maybe to the point of having butterflies in your stomach!

One of the main obstacles to overcome when we are about to set off on a bike tour is fear. Thoughts will be swirling in your head trying to convince you that it will be dangerous. It is a very common experience that can affect beginners as well as more experienced cyclists. I have felt it myself in the past, and even after years of touring when embarking on a new journey, there can be that moment of apprehension and doubt creeping in.

Why does one feel this way?

Let us consider some of the reasons why the simple thought of touring on a bicycle can bring some apprehension and even fear.

For most people the first bicycle tour is a break with convention. In modern times and in most cultures, we have become accustomed to a way of travelling, and indeed living, that relies on the expertise of others and brings us a sense of familiarity and safety. An entire industry is built around providing services that, at least in theory, remove all risks associated with tourism. It ranges from organised tours where all your needs are planned ahead and catered for, to seemingly more independent ways of travelling that are still dependent on a transport infrastructure, hotel or other accommodation bookings and a range of products and services that keep us comfortable. Of course there is nothing wrong with all this per se. For the majority, it is the most enjoyable way to experience a vacation. There is a negative consequence though; we have naturally become less able to be self reliant, to find our own solutions and adapt to any given situation. A bike tour, like a long hike, could be the first time we are thrusted into an activity where for the most part, we are 'on our own' so to speak, relying on our own strength for transport and our own resourcefulness to cope with the unpredictable circumstances each day can bring. Like a muscle we haven't used for a long time, it is only natural that a level of strength must be rebuilt before we can feel confident in our own abilities.

Next there is some fear associated with the intrinsic nature of travel, although this is also one of its main rewards. The further afield you go, the more you are confronted with the unknown; language, culture, customs, climates and landscapes might be very unfamiliar and bring some unease if not fear. In the connected world we now live in, we can be better prepared and informed, but only first hand experience will tell us how a certain place can affect us and how we will react.

Another aspect that contributes much to unfounded fears, is the way that the media depicts the world we live in. For the sake of capturing people's attention, a general trend is to highlight and blow out of proportion the bad news while, for the most part, leaving the good stories untold. Daily bulletins are filled with the gruesome and the ghastly, leaving the impression that the world must indeed be a dangerous place. One of the greatest discoveries and insights a journey can bring is the recognition that what you were told was mostly biased and one-sided and, with few exceptions, what you will find instead are examples of generosity, care, curiosity and hospitality that bind us together as human beings. Simple facts of life like these never quite make it into a news broadcast.

I believe that most of our fears, compounded by some of the factors above, are in the end imaginary and self-created. On a bicycle you are indeed more exposed to the landscape and people around you and this, at first, can make you feel more vulnerable but, provided that what you are planning is not reckless or completely out of your means, it is worth asking yourself a simple question:

Is doing what I love worth the small risks I will be taking?

Whether we are aware of it or not, we willingly take risks all the time. We might delude ourselves and pretend to live lives that are cautious, yet not a day goes by without having to take some risks. No matter where, whether you ride your bike or drive your car or walk for that matter, there is always a tiny chance of being in the wrong place at the wrong time. The alternative would be to spend our time isolated and protected by four walls sitting on a sofa, which by the way would be the worst thing you could do to your mental and physical health. I am not advocating an approach where one is completely unaware of the conditions that one will be facing; that would be equally foolish and unnecessary. Do all the research you can when you are planning your trip and become aware of the obstacles you are likely to be facing. Once again, the internet will be your friend. Read accounts of travelers that have recently taken a similar trip to get you more acquainted with what to expect. Should you visit countries with political and social situations you are not familiar with, do read your government's advice to know what they say and recommend to tourists. Bear in mind that, not unlike the news, even these reports are often skewed towards a cautious approach and can at times be much exaggerated.

Bike touring is a learning process. With experience will come resilience and the ability to have more trust in yourself and feel more relaxed in your surroundings. What experience has definitely taught me is that most fears are irrational and mostly unfounded; those worst case scenarios that keep you awake the night before your departure are extremely unlikely to become reality. Even if they were to occur, you would likely find the resilience to deal with them appropriately and successfully, no matter what they were. I can assure you that no event will ever be as dramatic as your thoughts and worries led you to believe in the first place.

Let me share a couple of examples from my own experience. The first one took place on a trip I took to western Canada. This was the first time that I had ever planned a tour in some rather remote locations that needed a few days riding between facilities. Before my departure I had the odd thought about having to face a bear in what was definitely grizzly territory! Once I arrived in Calgary and boarded a bus to Banff to get me to the starting point of my cycling, I felt in the grip of a different kind of fear. Looking out of the window I stared at the endless stretches of forest and wild rivers and quickly, thoughts turned into worries. What would happen if I got stuck somewhere like this? Would anyone stop and rescue me? What about if I was to run out of water and food? The following day I started pedaling. I ventured for a week into a more remote part than I had gone through on that bus journey; interestingly, once on the bicycle, not once did I feel afraid or threatened, and I loved every minute of it. Thoughts in the head often like building worst case scenarios, but it is our choice whether or not to believe in them.

A few years later, something else occurred that is a good example of how, even when unfortunate things occur, a solution is usually found. I was cycling in some remote parts of the Indian Himalayas with a good friend. We were approaching 5000 metres of altitude when, in the middle of nowhere, he started feeling rather poorly. For the first time he told me that his heart had been funny the previous night and that he had been struggling with his breathing. This was worse than I could have imagined months before when planning, but there was a difference. Then, I would have been worrying about it in the comfort of my bed, imagining how, in such a place, nobody might be found to assist us and how as a result the entire trip would go pear shaped. In reality, despite the serious consequences such an incident could have had, we took some quick decisions and dealt with it. There were no villages we could have reached in either direction. We decided to turn around and descend the mountain as much as possible, which made my friend's condition much better; next we decided the safest thing would be to wait for some help to come along the road and take him to a military hospital, which I knew by car was about six or seven hours ahead. It was getting dark and traffic was really sparse, but within about half an hour a couple of jeeps arrived and stopped. Despite being full, they understood the emergency and kindly made some space for him and his bike. Two days later we met again in the small village by the military hospital. He had been checked by a doctor, given some medicines for the altitude and told that he could continue provided he felt up to it. Luckily he did and we successfully completed the rest of our trip together.

To conclude, overcoming your fears is best done gradually, step by step like walking, but never let it stop you from doing the things you love or at least from trying. With experience you will gain in strength and confidence and all that will be left is a different and healthier kind of fear; the instinct that will tell you and warn you, each time you are facing real danger.

Transporting the bike

This is when having a folding bike brings the greatest advantage. Its small footprint will make it easier to carry from and to an airport or a station and you will have a wider choice of bags to fit it in easily.

As with any traditional touring bike, the main consideration is what kind of protection we would like for our bike. This seems straightforward, after all wouldn't we all choose the best and most secure way to transport it? As I will explain it is a little more complicated; the kind of luggage you use will affect to a certain extent the type of tour you will be able to take and could also impact on your expenses.

There are two main choices here:

- Hard Cases

- Soft Bags

Hard Cases

There is a good selection of hard cases to choose from on the market. More and more people like to carry their bikes with them on a holiday, whether they use them for touring or simply for daily rides. Hard cases are generally quite expensive, heavy and mostly designed to fit the bike tightly, without leaving much space for anything else. They use a hard shell that protects the bike from damage and have lots of padding on the inside to further protect the bike no matter what happens. They are also large and cumbersome, but on the plus side quite comfortable to move about, as they always include wheels in order to be rolled effortlessly.

Prices will vary greatly across brands, but as of writing the average price for such bags is in excess of 200 dollars, euros or pound sterling. To this initial investment you may have to add other expenses. Maybe you will use exclusively trains or buses, but if you were to travel on a plane instead, these sorts of cases will likely push you outside your luggage weight allowances and extra fees will apply. Airlines policies vary but often a bicycle falls into the 'sport equipment' category and extra charges might apply. There is another aspect to consider. As I mentioned earlier, these cases do not have much space left for anything else apart from the bike. This means that you will have to carry more weight in the cabin. Often airlines will not let you bring more than one bag as carry on luggage and will also want to know its weight. You see where this is going. Yet again more charges, as well as losing your patience in stressful negotiations! Furthermore, some items can be transported in your checked in luggage but are prohibited as carry on luggage. In this situation take good care that you are not carrying any sharp items, combustibles, bike tools or camping equipment that might be taken off you when you go through a security screening.

But wait, you might ask yourself:

"Haven't you mentioned the big advantage of folding bikes is their small footprint? Surely this will make a difference?"

Yes and no is the answer.

Even for an extremely compact folding bike like a Brompton, hard cases tend to be quite bulky and, as far as weight goes, almost as heavy as their larger cousins. The only real difference might be a shape that is more of a square than a rectangle, but the wheels, the thick hard shell, the padding and indeed your folding bike will be just as heavy. They are also similarly expensive and still won't let you put much else inside beyond the bike.

As far as affecting what kind of tour you will be able to take, a hard case poses also a practical problem. You will most likely not be able to take the case along with you as you cycle. If your tour starts and ends from the same location it shouldn't be hard to store it at a hotel where you could stay for a night and return once the journey is over. If your time is limited this would still have the minor inconvenience of forcing you to spend a couple of nights in a hotel instead of being able to set off cycling straight away. The main inconvenience though is the inability to plan a linear tour from point A to point B without having to take transportation in order to return to your starting point.

Provided the above conditions are not too limiting, a hard case will probably be a good choice that will give you peace of mind while ensuring that your bike will stay safe and undamaged.

Soft Bags

Their only real downfall is the fact that during transportation, especially by airplane, they are not as good as hard cases in protecting your bicycle. On the other hand they give you all the freedom to decide where to stay and how to travel. As soft bags are light and can be folded small and carried as part of your luggage, you will also have the ability to use them should you need to take a transfer in the middle of your journey. Soft bags come in all kinds of shapes and can be as cheap as a cup of coffee. Being light, they limit the chances of you having to pay any extra fees during transport, and this is compounded by the fact that, unlike a hard bike case, they don't 'scream' bicycle. They look more like standard luggage to staff that could get suspicious as to what you have stored inside. As they are not designed to contain the bicycle and don't have all the padding and extra protection that goes with it, they allow you to utilize all the rest of the space to pack items that would be otherwise harder to carry on the plane. You are then able to stuff in your tent, sleeping bag, sharp tools, some clothes or even an extra tyre and these will become your surrogate padding that protects your bike, which takes me to the next point.

The last thing we want as touring cyclists is to realise that our bike has been damaged during transport. With a soft bag one has to put in some extra care and limit this from happening in the first place. Besides stuffing the bag with soft items all around the bike, one thing that can be done is to place some extra soft padding at the bottom. A few sponges or similar soft material, will go some way to ensure that when the bag is put on the floor by baggage handlers it will have something to cushion any impact. Another good idea, as we are dealing with a soft bag, is to insert some cardboard that you can cut down to size in order to form a light makeshift shell that can protect the bike further.

Soft cases are all that I have used for all my touring travel. Experience has taught me how to compensate for their vulnerability by using some of the ideas I have just outlined.

Have I ever sustained any damage to the bike as a result?

In ten years of touring with a folding bike I have had a rear rack damaged a couple of times. Both times this was not something that prevented me from going ahead with what I had planned. This experience made me aware of the need to find some solutions to limit this from happening. The extra padding at the bottom of the bag was a result of this process; it has so far been successful and I haven't had a single instance of such a repeat accident.

Following the route

The route has been planned in more or less detail. Before departing, I like to create a pdf file on my phone or tablet with a breakdown of where I will be riding and all the information I have collected stage by stage. In order to follow my route what I need next is obviously a map.

If you are a paper-map-only kind of person, you should know how to read them properly and be able to navigate by following a compass or having a good sense of direction. While you can still navigate roads and lanes this way, the advent of GPS or Global Positioning System, installed in most smartphones, makes it very easy to follow a route. For the digitally inclined, myself included, it means simply downloading all the offline digital maps of the area I am going to visit so that I can access them without needing any connection to the internet. The GPS system on the phone will then display my positioning on the maps I have downloaded. This makes it extremely easy to navigate; when needed, a quick glance will tell me exactly where I am and the direction to take next. In some places you will have hardly any doubt as roads are few and far between, but in the maze of streets of any city you are not familiar with, it is much harder and makes the GPS function a very useful one to have. Beyond the ease of use compared to paper maps, digital maps can also be zoomed very close with a touch of a finger giving you the ideal resolution when you need to work things out.

For those who want to take it a step further, ensuring that they never miss a turn on the route they have planned, there are dedicated apps for smartphones as well as GPS gadgets that will guide you step by step by voice or visual display. They will save you some mistakes and backtracking here and there, but I personally find them overkill and don't use them for the following reasons. If using a smartphone, guidance apps will not work in airplane mode and the software's continuous need to work out your position is a drain on the battery. GPS devices have less flashy displays and, built just to carry out this function, are a bit more efficient when it comes to battery life, but you will have to carry one more gadget with its cables, charger and batteries that will need to be re-charged.

Where to stay

I briefly introduced this topic when I talked about the need to book accommodation in advance and mentioned how it can affect the type of tour you are planning and the level of comfort you seek when you are on a holiday. The kind of budget you are setting aside for your trip, as well as your preferences, will help you decide whether to spend all of your nights in hotels, guest houses, at campsites, wild camping or a mix of them all. Having at least an idea of where you are likely to stay is important when you are bike touring because it will determine what you need to carry; furthermore on a folding bike the ability to load a lot of weight is more limited than on touring bikes so a little more planning becomes necessary. I will now outline the main options as far as accommodation types are concerned, with an eye to their benefits and limitations when bike touring.

Hotels

In this category I include not only hotels but also any kind of facility offering rooms for one or more nights. These provide the safest and most comfortable stay. You will be able to store your bike and your luggage safely and, should you want to, have the option to eat on the premises, without having to spend time looking for food. Everyone appreciates the comfort of sleeping on a proper bed and no matter the season, adjust the temperature to one's liking. Especially after a long, hot day of cycling, being able to take a shower and feel refreshed is, together with large quantities of food, one of the most blissful times for any touring cyclist! Access to hot water or even laundry facilities will also mean that you will be able to rinse your clothes and have them dry and ready by the following morning. The rooms can be reserved and offer the relief of knowing in advance where you will stay, thus saving you time.

Should you need assistance there will be occasions when staff might be able to assist you or at least point you in the right direction.

If money was not an issue you might think this is the best option to choose from but there are some trade-offs to make and because of them this might not always be true for everybody. Let's look at some of the downsides of planning a tour where most if not all nights are spent in hotels.

Prices of course will vary according to the destination but for those wanting to tour on a budget, this is the most expensive way to travel, especially so if travelling solo. If touring with others this is less of a problem as it might be possible to share a room; doing so lowers the cost considerably and you might find that there is not much difference between a hotel stay and a tent spot at a campsite.

Relying on hotels very often means having to plan in advance where you will be staying, and usually making a reservation too. Doing so will somehow limit that freedom that is one of the things I appreciate most when bike touring. As you ride you might find a place you really like and wish you could spend more time exploring or even be able to stay for the night. If you have made a reservation elsewhere, this is not practical because cancelling on the same day usually means paying a full night's fee.

The ability to comfortably cycle long distances is affected by many things. Whether one has had a good night's rest, the fitness level, the kind of food one eats as well as the ability to keep well hydrated, the weather encountered and many more factors. These variables will never be the same. There will be days when reaching your goal will be easy and you wish you were able to continue further, and other days when you have hardly reached half way and feel exhausted. Without the flexibility to stop wherever you want, you won't be left with much choice but to push on further than you would like.

This was mentioned already, but with advance bookings there will be occasions when you realise that the place you reserved does not meet your expectations. By the time this happens it will be too late to cancel and you will have to put up with whatever you find. In places where there is a large choice of hotel rooms available, you could decide not to book anything in advance. This can sometimes work just fine but you will lose a bit of time searching for the right place to stay. Depending on the season you are travelling, you might also run into the occasional problem of discovering that all places within easy reach are fully booked.

Something else that is not an issue if travelling with another person or in a group, is the fact that I find hotels can, at times, feel rather isolating. Everyone will spend most of their time in their room when not out exploring, and this can make it a little harder to interact with local people as well as with fellow travellers.

Youth Hostels

An alternative when staying in cities, is to stay at a Youth Hostel instead. First it is worth mentioning that such establishments not only cater to young teenagers. Staying at any hostel, no matter where in the world, you will see how guests' ages can span across a wide range. Their quality and service can vary greatly, but they will offer some of the hotels' comforts for a much more reasonable price. Some hostels will require you to purchase a membership card to be able to stay, but these can be bought there and then for a nominal feel. The same card will allow you to stay in pretty much any other hostel and will be valid for the whole year. While they are mostly known for large dorms and facilities to be shared with several people, they also cater for guests who want individual rooms and more privacy.

Beyond price, what I have always enjoyed about hostels is the fact that they are geared towards the independent traveller and you will find common rooms full of people busy planning their next destination. Unlike hotels, you will find it easy to strike up a conversation and share tips on what the unmissable places are in the area. You will not get the 'five star hotel' attention to detail, but staff are otherwise mostly friendly and love to work in an atmosphere that is usually a melting pot of different cultures. Should you spend more than one night they normally also offer the chance to join in any free tours and all kinds of activities where you can have fun, meet new people and provide a diversion from the fun you have on the bike.

Youth hostels are mostly prevalent in large cities or touristic spots, but rarely available off-the-beaten track. They are also very popular, as well as limited in number, and will often require a reservation to be made well in advance.

Bed & Breakfast, Homestays or Guest Houses

How they are called varies in different places, as does their availability. They are mostly families or individuals who have one or more spare bedrooms available to tourists for rent. These can be either in the same house they live in or within easy reach of their main premises. For the most part they offer simple facilities with no frills at a competitive price that often includes a morning breakfast meal too.

These kinds of properties are found all over the world and together with camping are one of the staple accommodations for the touring cyclist. Some of them you might be able to find with a search online or even be able to book from an app on your mobile, but they are mostly found by chance along the way as you cycle. You discover them by asking people in a village or town, as well as keeping an eye out for a signpost or a placard stuck on the outside of a front door. Unlike the word 'hotel', which is pretty much recognised internationally, their name in the local language can sound completely alien. Before you depart, do a little research and learn how to call them in the local language so that you will be able to ask for advice when you are looking for one.

They might be lacking the comfort and privacy that a hotel can offer but, unlike hotels, you will have the wonderful opportunity to get to know your hosts and get an insight, even if only for a few hours, into the lives of people in the country. Very often you will find hosts who know the area like the backs of their hands and will be eager to suggest the best roads to take the following day or the best restaurant to stop at.

Campsites

For those who want to feel closer to nature during their bike tours, campsites are arguably the best choice. If you are happy to spend nights in a tent sacrificing a little comfort, you will be able to experience the outdoors like you wouldn't be able to otherwise. Ubiquitous in most parts of the world, campsites are also one of the most economic options available. Camping culture and popularity differ from country to country and this will be reflected in the quality of services and facilities that you will find. At their most basic you should be able to find at least water, toilet facilities and electricity outlets. I have already talked about the benefits of carrying camping equipment and, unless one is touring in densely populated and touristic destinations, it is something that I recommend.

In protected areas such as National Parks or Nature Reserves a basic campsite might be the only facility where tourists can stay. Touring in such areas without a tent can prevent the chance to experience nature at its best as you would be forced to move on in search of hotels and facilities that only a town or at least a village can offer. Camping in cold seasons or in rain-prone areas brings its own challenges; be realistic about what is feasible and always test in advance the quality of your equipment, ensuring it withstands the conditions you are likely to encounter. Throughout years of cycling experience it is worth pointing out that I have only once been turned away from staying in a 'full' campsite. It was most unusual and due to a very busy weekend on a National Holiday in the US. If you mention you are touring on a bicycle, almost without fail a small corner will be usually found to put up your tent.

Wild Camping

This is also sometimes referred to as 'Stealth Camping', a term I don't particularly like, since it has a sneaky connotation. If you have done some bike touring before and carry a tent, chances are that this is something you are already familiar with. Whether one is stuck somewhere and left with no other option or one is deliberately doing it to cut down on expenses, carrying a tent offers the ultimate freedom that comes from knowing that wherever you might find yourself there is the possibility to stop and pitch the tent for the night. A simple definition could be: 'Camping anywhere with a tent to get some rest'. When camping in general, but even more so when wild camping, the main rule to follow is to always respect nature. Those of us who travel into the wilderness share the responsibility of helping to preserve it. Always follow a 'Leave No Trace' etiquette as the best way to respect wild spaces. Make sure you collect food leftovers and litter in order to dispose of them at a suitable place.

One of the main concerns about wild camping is whether it is legal in the first place. Rules vary from country to country, but provided one doesn't trespass onto private land and follows some simple advice this is rarely a problem. Let's have a look at some tips worth considering in order to do it safely.

The best advice when considering spending the night wild camping is to start looking for a suitable place ahead of time. One hour before stopping and in daylight, start to scan around the area you are cycling in to search for the best spot you can find. Leaving it late when it gets too dark will make it more likely that you make a mistake and pitch your tent somewhere ill advised. What should one look for in the first place?

- ❖ Somewhere secluded and unseen from the road but still within easy access.

- ❖ Somewhere away from trails or signs of frequent passage.

- ❖ Somewhere within reach of water unless you are carrying enough.

There are other things to consider. If possible choose a place on higher ground than the road; people passing by, especially in cars, will tend to look up much less than looking down. Also lower ground is more likely to collect water if there is a heavy rainfall and staying higher up will make it less likely that you wake up in a tent that is floating! For the same reason avoid any ground that is hollow. Talking from experience, be wary of pitching next to river beds, especially when in a narrow valley or in the mountains. Flash floods can be extremely dangerous and, in bad weather, can turn a small stream into a gushing river much quicker than you might think.

The idea is to find one or more suitable places within a short distance and, once a decision is made, wait until it starts getting dark. This lapse of time will give you some good clues. Were there people passing by? Has anyone spotted you or is it as quiet as you expected it to be? If nobody was around at dusk and you don't see any other signs of frequent passage, it is highly unlikely that anybody will turn up once night falls.

After you pitch your tent still remember to be unobtrusive and don't highlight your presence with loud sounds or excessive lights, and avoid lighting a fire. Chances are you will sleep early and wake up before dawn, which is the ideal time to pack up your tent and move on, completely unnoticed.

If you find yourself in an area with farms and fenced land the best tactic is to ask first. See if you can spot a farmer while cycling and simply ask if he would mind you pitching your tent on his land for the night. Mentioning you won't leave a trace and will depart early the following morning should help getting a positive response; after all they normally don't lack space! Never go into a fenced area without this prior consent. You could upset livestock or end up with an upset farmer chasing you out in the middle of the night or early morning.

The suggestions above are most relevant in uninhabited spaces or in the countryside. Free camping in an urban area needs much more caution because you are unlikely not to be spotted by someone. As a general rule consider stocking up on food and drinks, and move on further until you find a quieter place. When this is not possible and you are not able to find a room or a campsite, asking is again the best approach to take.

In some parts of the world police or fire brigade stations are a good place to start. Sometimes they might offer you a patch of grass on their premises and even when they don't, they are the best people to advise you on a good and safe place where you could pitch your tent. I have also spent nights on restaurants' lawns and in pub gardens. I would usually ask by mentioning that I would love to eat there but I also need to find a place to put my tent for the night. Knowing you are willing to spend some of your money on their premises might land you an invitation or at least a good suggestion. When everything else fails some of the safest places in villages or towns are churchyards and cemeteries. It sounds morbid and not for the faint hearted, but these usually offer some sheltered corners and are some of the least likely places where people would take a stroll at night.

In order to be able to pitch a tent on any kind of ground I have already mentioned that a freestanding tent is the best choice. Another good idea is to choose tents that don't have brightly coloured flysheets, as these are less likely to go unnoticed. If possible, choose tents with subdued colours that don't stick out as much in the landscape.

Wild camping, like bike touring, takes a little getting used to. Initially there are the subconscious fears of being somewhere unknown, feeling isolated and in the dark; these are all things that play on our most elemental fears. If looked at rationally though, provided you have followed some of the common-sense advice I have given, they are exactly the same reasons why you are much safer than you would imagine. Chances of encountering an ill-intentioned individual in a remote forest at night are highly exaggerated and mostly experienced while watching some Hollywood horror films.

Another subconscious fear that will likely play on our imaginations is the possibility of encountering some threatening wildlife. This too is extremely unlikely but, depending on where you are, some consideration must be given to the wildlife around you. Prior to travelling, do some research and learn if this is something that can pose a concern. If it is, learn the things you should do in order to keep safe at all times. One of the most common examples of this is camping in bear territory. In such places, sticking to a few simple rules is enough to avoid a chance encounter. The most important rule to follow when dealing with animals in open spaces is to never keep food or any other scents inside the tent as this is the only thing that might attract them. If you are cooking your meal or eating, do so in a different place, away from the spot where you will be camping. Store all food, toiletries and anything that has a scent at a distance; a common technique in such situations is to store such stuff in bags tied to a rope looped around some high tree branches.

With a little experience the initial jitters you might feel when wild camping will likely become less and less, and you will be left with the confidence and freedom that comes from knowing that no matter where you find yourself there is always a good place to get some rest.

How to pack the luggage

We have already discussed the options available when it comes to carrying the luggage. What this section will describe instead is how to best distribute what you are carrying. This is how I do it, but with some experience chances are that you will find a way that works better for you, so take all these tips as simple suggestions.

Assuming you are using two main bags, as I was suggesting earlier, how you distribute your luggage should follow three considerations: weight distribution, convenience and safety.

Weight distribution is important when bike touring as it affects the bike handling as well as the strain you place on its different parts. Because your body weight puts most of the stress on the rear wheel it makes sense to keep the rear luggage as light as possible. In my setup the rear backpack has more volume than the front bag but most of its space is filled by things of large volume but little weight such as spare clothes, tent, down sleeping bag, camping mattress and pillow, a pair of light sleepers and the empty bags I have used to carry the bike in. The front bag, although smaller, is reserved for heavier items, of course always bearing in mind the recommended weight limitations. This distribution shifts some of the load towards the front, making even a folding bike with small wheels much less twitchy and therefore more stable and easy to ride.

What I mean by convenience is the fact that I store things in such a way that the items I frequently use during the day are stored in the front bag, which gives me a much easier access. I normally cover my backpack at all times with a raincover to protect it in case of rain, but also from dirt and dust on sunny days. The fact that it is covered, together with its location at the rear of the bike, makes it much harder to reach and open should I need something, and indeed this cannot be done without stopping and leaning the bike somewhere. Instead, all I need to reach the front bag, is to stop and stretch an arm to open it, with no need to dismount from the bike. For this reason all the gadgets I regularly use are stored here. That's where I put all filming equipment, as well as the phone I use for pictures and guidance, portable batteries and solar panel and cables I might need. Similarly, toiletries, water and food I am having during the day, and a rain jacket and sweater to quickly adapt to changes in temperature.

The order I stack things, especially in the backpack, is also according to frequency of use. The bags to carry the bike on a plane or a train for example, are normally only used twice, to transport the bike; as they are not used during the bike tour itself, they are put at the bottom of the pile. The same goes for tools and spares to repair the bike, in the hope that they will not have to be used!

Thirdly, an important consideration is safety. I will explore bike safety in more depth in a later section, but for now it is enough to say that inevitably there will be times when you have to park and lock your bike in order to do some sightseeing or buy groceries. It is not practical to always unload all the bags when having to do this. The idea is to only carry one of them with you, ensuring it contains the most essential things such as valuables, documents and money. In my case this is again the front bag, as it is much easier and faster to remove from the bike. All I need to do is to pull a lever to remove it from the front block that it is attached to and with ease I am able to bring it with me. The front bag is also the obvious choice for storing valuables because your eyes are always on it. If you forget to secure something or close a zipper it is much less likely that you will lose things without noticing and in crowded situations when dealing with people you will be much more aware and able to protect your valuables.

Riding a folding bike

In case you are intimidated by the title, I promise I won't talk about the physics of balance or ask you to install some stabiliser wheels to get you started! However, I still feel a short section to point out the differences in the way you ride a folding bike as opposed to a regular bike are worth mentioning. If you are used to normal bikes there will be some adjustments to make and I recommend, before you depart, to get well acquainted with the most obvious ones. A few practice rides will give you a feel for what you need to pay more attention to and what feels awkward and different.

Starting with the most obvious one, ensure that you are thoroughly familiar with the folding system of the bike. This usually involves a set of clamps or latches that need to be secured in order for the bicycle to be safely ridden. Practice folding and unfolding it frequently so that it becomes something you are well accustomed to. I find the most important advice is to be aware at all times that you are riding on wheels that are likely to be 20" or even as small as 16". Hitting a rock or a pothole on a mountain bike with wide and thick tyres is hardly noticed, while with such tiny wheels the same obstacle can easily cause a fall.

It won't be a problem when you are slowly climbing a hill and less likely to happen on a flat road, but when going downhill and generally at fast speeds, much more focus and attention is needed.

Another characteristic of folding bikes, again due to the small wheels, is the fact that when steering they can feel rather twitchy. Usually a little experience riding them will help your body adjust automatically, and after some time this shouldn't be a problem anymore. I have also noticed how a folding bike loaded with the weight of some luggage, has a tendency to become much more stable and to neutralise this.

Be aware that small wheels will have a slight impact on your brakes and possibly downgrade their power. It has never been an issue personally, but I have read accounts of brake pads overheating during fast descents, due to the small wheels spinning faster. Some folding bikes come equipped with the latest technology, and if yours has hydraulic disk brakes this would of course not be a problem.

Provided one is aware of these small differences and makes the necessary adjustments, folding bikes can be ridden as safely as any other kind of bike. When in doubt, or not completely familiar with your folder yet, err on the side of caution and be a little more prudent than you would be otherwise, and all will be fine.

Food and Water

Eating and rehydrating adequately is key to feeling comfortable during the long days of cycling that any bike tour demands. Any cyclist will have experienced how hard it is to pedal when thirsty or with a stomach that feels empty. One becomes quickly exhausted, with no energy to spare, and even covering a short distance feels like torture. Regarding food, a rough estimate is to consider that for every kilometre cycled you will have an additional calorie need of about 30 calories so assuming a 100 kilometres distance covered in a day you will need to replenish 3000 extra calories. This means that for once the main concern is to pile up calories; you can eat to your heart's content and, by the end of it, be lighter than the day you started the trip! As far as fluids go, the latest research recommends drinking enough to satisfy your thirst. What the liquid intake should be is highly variable depending on temperature, intensity of the ride, and other factors such as body size and so on.

In order to carry the minimum weight I can, I do not bring any cooking equipment. This is a personal preference though and I know that for some, the ability to cook or brew some coffee or a cup of tea while camping is essential. If you are one of these, you will need to reserve the space to accommodate the utensils and stove that are necessary but also space to carry ingredients, spices and fats that are needed for cooking. Depending on the cooking system you bring, ensure that the appropriate fuel is also available for purchase wherever you are visiting because flammable items won't be accepted as luggage on an airplane. I find that my 'no cooking' policy is only a limitation in some remote places where you don't have access to food and restaurants for several days. When I have found myself in such circumstances I have put up with cold meals that, if not as satisfying taste-wise, were still more than adequate to provide the energy that was necessary. All I carried was a good screw top container that was leak-proof, together with bags of oats, grains, nuts and dried fruit, plus packaged food such as biscuits, peanut butter, chocolate spreads or jams. A few hours before my main meal I would put some oats into the sealed container and let them soak in cold water as I was riding or during the night. After a few hours they absorb the water and get to a soft consistency that makes them more edible, and you are able to mix them with some nuts, or peanut butter or fruits, or a syrup to add nutrients and taste. Bags of oats are some of the lightest and most nutritious food you can carry so, as drab as it sounds, this works and will keep you healthy and able to cope with your cycling. Most of the time, chances are that you will be able to get a warm meal or even two during the day as you cycle; and as for snacks, carry biscuits, chocolate bars or whatever you might fancy.

Calorie consumption still needs to be tailored to the fact that you will be exercising. What I have always found works best for me is to start the day with a nutritious breakfast. Once you start cycling the best way to keep up your energy levels and your performance is to stop frequently for small snacks and smaller meals with low fats but high in carbohydrates rather than filling up on a large lunch that will take time to digest and will make you feel sluggish. At the end of the day you can further indulge in a big meal that will restore your energies and prepare you for the following day. In a similar way, when hydrating, consider frequent sips of water that your body can process more effectively rather than binging only a few times during the day. I am not a nutritionist but food, beyond some basic considerations, doesn't need to be too much of a concern on a bike tour, unless you are trying to reach peak performance or break some records. Exploring food and drink after all is part of the whole excitement of a journey and all one has to take care of is that it is done sensibly.

The most important thing is to know where you will find supplies of water and food along the route you are following. This is why doing some prior research can be helpful. Knowing whether on a particular day you will be passing plenty of places to get food and water or whether there will not be even one, will help you take the best approach. Do also take care about the quality of food and water that is available in a given place. Often tap water quality that we usually take for granted in our homes is not safe to drink, at least for non-local tourists; here, well-sealed bottled water will be the only option. In such places even harmless foods like fruit and vegetables washed with the tap water will end up causing stomach trouble. For the same reason anything that contains ice cubes is better avoided. The level of sanitation in a country can also affect food quality and, as we need to be in good health in order to be able to cycle, more precautions than normal should be taken. If you are touring areas where you think that this may be a problem, stick as far as possible to freshly cooked meals and limit yourself to fruit and vegetables that you can peel yourself.

In some situations, especially when touring more remote locations where water cannot always be bought, it makes a lot of sense to bring a purifying system or some tablets. For simplicity I prefer the latter. A small and extremely light packet of 50 tablets will purify 50 litres of water for those times when you have no other option. An advantage of tablets is that they are really easy to use and all you need to do is dissolve one in a litre of water and let it rest for 30 minutes to 2 hours depending on the manufacturers.

It is often necessary to store open food when you are not eating it all at the same time and for this I always bring some transparent, sealable plastic pouches that can also be used to store light rubbish.

Hygiene

A frequently asked question is how does a cyclist manage to keep clean and presentable when touring? The answer could be 'easily' or 'badly' and everything in between. Hopefully the latter is short term and forced by unwelcoming conditions that are found in places most cyclists tend to avoid. Keeping clean is a function of the how, where and when you travel. If you like your comforts and are staying in hotel rooms night after night this is a non issue. It gets more challenging when this is not possible as facilities are bare or non-existent or if you have chosen to wild camp most of the time. Even in these situations there are a few things that can be done to at least maintain a basic level of cleanliness. Keeping clean involves using chemicals and waste-disposal. In our homes we have facilities to manage these but this is not the case in the wilderness. That's why you need to educate yourself about the kinds of personal care products you can bring with you and how to use them and dispose of them responsibly. When you know you will be spending days without having access to disposal facilities, limit your waste as you will have to carry it until you find them. Always have a suitable stock of sealable plastic bags; they are not the most environmentally friendly but are extremely light and at least allow you to carry all waste in a clean and secure way.

The easiest way to maintain bodily cleanliness when water is not available or temperatures are too uncomfortable to get wet, is to come equipped with wet tissues or baby wipes. Baby wipes are best as they are intended to keep skin clean and have less aggressive chemicals in them. Once your cycling is done for the day, by using them it is possible to clean your body while staying dry and sheltered in the comfort of your tent. According to some reports, wet wipes could take up to one hundred years to biodegrade and are well known for clogging pipes and drains. Limit their use to what is strictly necessary and always dispose of them responsibly. You're more likely to pick up a stomach bug if you forget to wash your hands, especially after using the toilet and when you're handling food. During the day a simple way to keep your hands clean is to carry a small bottle of alcohol sanitiser or hand cleaning gel.

In mild or warmer climates you will sweat more, and nothing compares to a proper rinse with soap and water. Remember those sponges you used to protect the bike when packing? I am all for things that have more than one use, and if able to find a secluded space, having a sponge and as little as a litre of water is enough to get a good rinse, while without one it would be challenging. Ideally use biodegradable soap as it will have less of an impact on nature. As far as towels are concerned, you will find plenty of small and light versions that are specifically designed for the outdoors and are made of quick-drying materials. For the smallest and lightest I have found that the best choice is chamois leather which I have been using for many years. This material, more commonly used for wiping windows dry, is excellent because a small patch can be twisted and dried in a matter of seconds. When choosing a place, take into consideration that to dispose safely of excess soapy water on the ground, it is recommended that 50 metres distance from any waterways is maintained.

It would be hard to keep clean without taking care of the clothes you are wearing while exercising for weeks. When I was talking about the equipment I carry I mentioned the amazing qualities of Merino wool. It is self cleaning and doesn't hold smells or odours, as the creatine in the wool naturally breaks down any bad smelling bacteria from the skin. Materials like this will allow you to use them a few more days than you normally would. Beyond that, the fact that you are carrying a full set of clothes to change into allows you the time to wash what you have worn for a few days and let it dry during the night or on the bike as you ride, by tying it on the outside of your bags, exposed to the heat of the sun. One item that I like to keep clean at all times is my underpants; as I am spending long hours on the saddle, this item will really benefit from a more frequent routine of washing and drying. By choosing a thin and light drying material, having two underpants is all you need. In the evening I use one as a sponge if I have the luxury to take a shower and wash it with the soap or shampoo I carry. Otherwise I do the same using a little water that I am carrying. At night I can wear a clean pair which I then use the following day. The washed pair has usually dried by the morning, but even if not completely dry you will have the rest of the day to let it dry tied somewhere on the bike. To wash and rinse clothes all you need is a small sink and the same shampoo you use for your hair and body will be adequate for the task. Do carry a good length of rope that can be used as a clothesline. The main challenge when washing garments that you will use the following day, is the fact that you will need to ensure they are dry before you start cycling in the morning. Space to tie them on the bike is limited and doing so they could get lost or damaged. If you are short of time one possible way around the problem is to wear them. This of course works only when they are damp but almost dry and is best done when you are touring in hot weather and you know it will be sunny.

The ultimate way of washing your clothes is to spend one hour or so at a laundrette facility where for a few coins you can use washing machines and spin dryers that will come in handy should your down sleeping bag or down jacket need a little drying and fluffing up after a few humid nights camping. Take advantage of these to wash your sleeping liner too. Some of my best memories of bike touring are indeed linked to such blissful places, and I am planning an ultimate world launderette guidebook for the near future! You can charge your gadgets while waiting; they might even have wifi, and often elderly ladies who will be keen to show you all the tricks for best using the machines or may provide some spare washing powder. You can also make the most of the time it takes for your laundry to be ready and invest in a good meal at a restaurant.

When nature calls and you are far from any facilities you will hopefully be able to spot a decent bush to take cover behind; harder for women than for men, but usually when this is necessary you are in places that are not crowded. Ideally, when it comes to poop, one should dig a hole and then cover it with soil, but for this you will need to have come equipped with a trowel. When bike touring in places with few opportunities to stop at restaurants or cafés to use their washrooms, bringing a roll of biodegradable toilet paper is only second in importance to bringing the bicycle! Carry a roll of thin light plastic bags to store used toilet paper in and dispose of it as soon as a suitable bin can be found.

Understanding the language

Ideally, the ability to speak some of the local language will bring lots of advantages and open doors that would otherwise remain shut. You can often get much better interactions with locals when you can start a conversation in their language. Learning languages can be a long, daunting task though, and it is absolutely possible to go ahead and travel in places where communication is going to be a challenge. When this happens, human nature, curiosity and a lot of laughter are ways to get by and can provide some very good stories and memories to recall. You may have to get used to being more expressive with your hands; a good idea could be to carry a notebook filled with phrases that could be read out or shown. For the artistically inclined the same notebook could be even used to draw something that you want to convey. The very least one can do is to learn the basic greetings, something that shouldn't take too much time or practice. Using local greetings, you are more likely to get a smile from the person you are addressing, and you will have demonstrated your interest in the local culture through such small efforts.

For most, getting by with a decent level of English, the current lingua franca, is the main solution to communication in most parts of the world, probably followed by the Spanish language. For anyone passionate about world travel, it is definitely worth the time and effort it takes to master these languages at least to a level that is understandable without needing to be perfect.

It has to be said that technology nowadays spoils us with a plethora of phone apps or dedicated gadgets where multiple languages are stored and can be translated with audio or text on the spot. They still have some way to go before being perfect but they do allow you to ask complicated sentences and translate an answer that is read out into your own language.

Other apps are fully dedicated to deciphering the most obscure writing. For a foreigner travelling in places where a different alphabet or scripts are used these can be a great help when trying to understand the names of towns or facilities written on otherwise mysterious signposts.

Maintenance and Repairs

A well maintained bicycle with good quality components is the best warranty against having to carry out repairs when touring. Unless you are qualified and competent enough to be able to check all parts and fix your bicycle yourself, maintenance starts with regular visits to a bike shop where you can get your bike serviced. Although I am able to fix some of the main issues that would stop me from riding, I never leave on a tour without taking the bike for a thorough check at my trusted Brompton dealer. Mentioning you are about to go on a tour should be enough for them to know what needs most paying attention to. A bike service will include a thorough inspection of the bike and replacement of parts that are most vulnerable to wear and tear such as wheels, chain, sprockets, brake pads and cables. Truing the wheels and checking the integrity of the rims will greatly reduce the likelihood of a failure that in some cases could stop you from continuing. They will also fine tune and adjust your brakes and gears and lubricate parts that most need it.

What I also normally do is be proactive in replacing worn parts rather than waiting for them to fail. As far as possible I keep track of the mileage done by each part and follow manufacturers' recommendations. Parts such as a bottom bracket or a hub gear system, if present, are not as easy to check for wear and tear but are obviously subject to it. Replacing something before it fails might seem wasteful at first, but you have to remember that folding bikes' parts are not usually available where you travel and such failures could force you to halt and make it hard to continue. Depending on the size and weight of the component you could also decide to carry the old part with you as a spare should a replacement become necessary.

As for other maintenance issues and repairs that might be needed whilst touring, you could invest some time learning how to fix at least some of the most common failures. In order of frequency I would say that punctures are the most likely to occur, and possibly they will be the only repairs you will have to deal with; and for this reason I will talk about this specific topic in more detail a little later. Next might be changing a worn tyre, tuning a brake or replacing worn brake pads or adjusting the gear shifting mechanism. For those seeking greater peace of mind it is a good idea to learn to fix some of the rarer failures such as replacing a gear or shifter cable, fixing a broken spoke or a broken chain.

These skills are best learnt in the comfort of your own home as they do take some practice to get right; as part of the learning process, there might also be occasions when you mess things up in a way that requires some fixing and further advice from a professional bike mechanic. Clearly if left to the last minute or dealt with on a foreign road without much help, such events have the potential to bring unnecessary stress and complications. Having some practice and getting to know the bike before you depart is also good advice because you will learn which tools are necessary for carrying out repairs on your specific bicycle. Beyond what is obvious such as lubrication oil, a pump, tyre levers and puncture repair patches, you will know exactly what sizes of allen key and wrenches you need to deal with repairs of components. A chain-breaker and a spoke wrench should also be included as they are small and light tools that could be extremely useful.

Next there is the important topic of which spares to take if any. You have already heard it many times before because it is that important! Folding bikes often have proprietary parts that are not available for sale in regular cycling stores. Something as simple as a good quality tyre for 16" or 20" wheels that are standard on folding bikes, might be extremely hard to source in most countries. Instead you will be offered tyres intended for children's bikes that are likely to last but a few days. Depending on the length of your tour, but also the quality of the roads you ride on, bringing a spare tyre is a good idea and something I always do. Do not depart for a tour with tyres that are worn out. Rather keep one worn out tyre for an emergency replacement and fit two new tyres before you start.

As for the rest, bring spare parts that are small and light enough to be carried such as brake pads, spare spokes for the front and rear wheels (that often come in different sizes), a couple of brake or gear cables, a few chain links, as well as any other parts that from experience you know could be vulnerable. These will depend on the bicycle you own.

Do not only carry things according to what you are able to repair. Even if it is true that a bike mechanic might not have a spare part for a folding bike or even might not be used to repairing one in the first place, chances are that with his expertise and the correct spare you can provide, he will be able to help you get back on the road safely.

If you follow the principles and ideas I have just highlighted, you will be able to complete the entire trip on a reliable bike that is very unlikely to let you down.

There is just one more thing...cyclists' worst enemies: punctures! They stop you from riding, delay you and get your hands dirty. As for the latter, I never depart for a trip without a pair of DIY gloves or some disposable vinyl gloves. They are so small, light and useful that they should always find a place in your repairs toolbox. Although punctures are part and parcel of cycling and impossible to avoid completely, here are 3 tips that can greatly help in reducing their occurrence.

❖ Tyre Wear:

I have already advised against setting off with worn tyres. When their treads get thin or start displaying many cuts in their rubber surface they are also much more likely to cause frequent punctures. The small circumference of folding bike wheels and the speed at which they are turning will wear down tyres faster than on larger bikes, especially on the rear wheel. For this reason it becomes important to check the quality of the tread more regularly in order to assess when a tyre change is needed.

❖ Air Pressure:

Investing money in a good portable pump is worth every penny. Maintaining the ideal tyre pressure with the average quality hand pump is hard if not impossible. Most hand pumps are designed for nothing more than getting you home if you need to fix a puncture, but won't let you bring up the pressure to the level recommended. Better quality portable hand pumps make this possible and without too much effort. While costing a little more money, they allow you to top up the air every couple of days, ensuring that the best pressure is always maintained; this has an important impact in reducing punctures, especially in the rear wheel which supports most of the weight and stress during a bike tour.

❖ Tyre Checks

Before you start your ride each day or at the end of it, get into the habit of spinning both wheels slowly to check if anything has got stuck to the tread. A sharp object doesn't always cause an immediate flat tyre; what often happens is that it slowly pierces into the rubber as you ride. If not sharp enough to puncture your inner tube, it might still cause small cuts on the tyre surface, which then is more likely to pick up further debris. Making this inspection a regular habit will highlight how worn the tyre is, which brings us back to the first point.

Keeping your bike safe

A cyclist's worst nightmare on a tour is having the bike stolen. While a touring bike loaded with heavy bags is cumbersome to deal with by ill-intentioned individuals, as much care as possible should be taken; after all it is your main means of transport, and furthermore may be carrying some of your important belongings. I have never had to deal with such an issue, but have read accounts of people who have experienced it.

If touring with a friend or in a group a lot of the advice I offer here is not necessary. In such circumstances all it takes is to plan stops so that at least one person is able to watch the bikes while the others are away. It is more of a challenge, though, when touring solo. Inevitably, there are times when you have to leave the bike unattended, whether for some grocery shopping, sightseeing, a quick stop at a café, a meal at a restaurant or overnight. While it is impossible to reduce the risk completely, I will share some tips that I have found useful and discuss how to keep your bike as safe as possible even when left unattended. A good thing about folding bikes is that they can be folded small and taken along rather than having to lock them. When touring with luggage attached to the bike though, this is not always practical or even possible. Having to remove bags and carry the bike along with you each time you stop would be most inconvenient. A good strategy is to follow 3 main points instead:

❖ Lock it

Don't forget the obvious! There are more or less secure locks on the market that vary greatly in price and weight. The more expensive ones will usually give some peace of mind but even the best can be compromised by a 'skilled' individual determined to steal your bike. The more secure, the heavier they are and the less compact. Always bring a lock that offers a good compromise and make it a habit to lock your bike at all times, even when you are not planning to leave it for long and might be tempted to not bother.

❖ Limit the times it is left unattended

If you are relying on grocery shopping for your drinks and meals, as a way to limit the risk, buy all you need for that day in one place rather than stopping multiple times. When I am staying in hotels or renting a room for the night, I always take advantage of the opportunity to fold the bike and take it inside with me. Unlike regular bikes, carrying a folded bike into your room will usually raise fewer eyebrows. Where this isn't possible make sure staff can offer a secure place where it can be stored and if they don't, consider staying somewhere else. When I am camping I can store my folded Brompton hidden under the tent flysheet. If you have to leave it on the outside, lock it safely to some structure and as a further measure, at night, tie one of the tent guidelines around the bike; doing so will give you warning if someone tries to tamper with it.

One of the pleasures of travel is to spend some time sightseeing. While a bike will enable you to move quickly around a town or a city, it can become a hindrance at times when you want to visit the interior of buildings or museums. There are ways you can deal with this. If a particular place offers a lot of sightseeing opportunities, consider booking a room rather than staying at a campsite. This way you will be able to use the bike when appropriate but also take the opportunity to store it, feeling free to enjoy the sightseeing without having to worry. If, on the other hand, I am simply passing through a place but want to stop and visit a sight in between cycling, I first of all check with reception staff if there is a place where I can lock my bike safely. If there isn't or I am not satisfied with what is suggested, a good idea is to find a café or a restaurant nearby that offers a secure place to lock it. Simply tell them that you would like to do some sightseeing before having a meal and ask if they would mind you leaving the bike somewhere safe on their premises. Usually this is enough to build some trust with the staff, who may offer a helpful solution knowing that you will become their customer later. Another option when entering a building is to ask if by chance you can park the bike somewhere inside. This is often not possible but you never know and asking is the only way to find out. As far as possible, stop in places where you can park your bike in such a way that it is visible from the inside. Stores with large windows are the obvious candidates as every now and then you can keep an eye on your bike.

❖ Be aware of your surroundings

Do not rush. Before locking the bike take some time to scan your surroundings and people around. After you lock it, walk some distance while keeping an eye on the bike, noticing whether it is drawing unwanted attention. A minute or two will be enough to give you a good idea of how safe it is going to be if left there a little longer. If you have a choice, plan to stop in small villages rather than larger towns or cities. In an urban area, avoid locking your bike in a place that is either too quiet or extremely crowded, as well as in places that are dark and secluded, out of sight from you as well as passers by.

A further measure I take when having to leave my bike unattended for any length of time is to add the further security of a bike alarm system. Nowadays, these are light, affordable, compact and readily available on the market. The particular one that I carry, costs about 15 euros or dollars, is powered by standard batteries and comes with a remote control. When I need to lock the bike, I put this gadget on standby and store it hidden in one of the pockets of my backpack that is left on the rear rack of the bike; any slight movement on the bike triggers a very loud siren that has a long range and can only be deactivated by the remote control I carry. If the bike is slightly moved or touched while the device is active, a loud alarm sound is triggered; a thief might still try to run away with the bike, but with the warning one has the chance to set up a good chase. Also the loud sound will probably take the person by surprise and chances are that he will give up trying in the first place.

Keeping gadgets charged

When touring on your folding bike you are likely to be carrying several gadgets. You will have at least a mobile phone, but maybe also a camera or an action camera, a drone as well as other electronic gadgets that need charging. If all you have is a mobile phone, chances are that it is a crucial part of enabling you to tour effectively. I use mine for pretty much everything while touring. It stores my offline maps, it shows my GPS position, it is used for communication, to manage bookings, for filming and photography and much more. Running out of power on something that is so important and helpful is not a tragedy but, as far as possible, something best avoided.

If you are mostly staying in hotels all you need are adaptors that fit with the local power outlets and the cables needed to charge everything at the end of the day. If, every now and then, you are wild camping or spend longer than a day without overnight access to electricity, it becomes necessary to find alternative ways. When needing to save power on mobile phones a simple trick which goes a long way, is to put the device into airplane mode, using it only when strictly necessary. Another thing one can do, if at all possible, is to plan a couple of lengthy stops for meals or at a café, asking whether you can plug in your devices. It won't be enough time to fully recharge them but will at least allow you to stretch their use a little.

When planning for such situations it is wiser to bring along one or even two power bank batteries that can be charged when you have the opportunity to do so and will then be able to provide enough output to recharge your devices several times over. The next step, and an even better solution, is to have a system that recharges the power bank batteries even at times when you don't have access to any outlets. The two most common ways to do so are by using portable solar panels or installing a hub dynamo.

I use the former as it is simpler and doesn't need any modifications on the bike. **(fig.26)** While cycling I attach the solar panels with two carabiners to the front bag and open them on the top in such a way that the cells face upwards, towards the sky. The cable attached to them is then plugged directly into the battery pack that sits in a pocket in the same bag. An entire day of cycling, especially in sunny conditions, normally refills the battery enough to allow charging of several devices in a process that can be repeated day after day. Hub dynamo chargers are also a good alternative that work even better than solar panels when weather conditions are poor;

~ (fig. 26) ~

on the downside, they are more expensive and need a new hub to be fitted on the front wheel for them to work.

With both systems it is best to use a powerbank as a buffer and resist the temptation to plug in your devices directly. A hub dynamo will not be able to charge consistently below certain speeds and the same goes for a solar panel when you are moving between areas of sun and shade. These surges and sudden drops in power can easily damage your gadgets in the process.

Documenting your trip

Something I personally do enjoy while bike touring is documenting the trip. This could be simply done for yourself, to share with family and friends or to share on social media. It might not be everybody's cup of tea and there is a fair argument that the best way to enjoy a journey is to avoid the distraction of wanting to capture it through a lens. Like with most things, I feel this criticism applies mostly when overdoing it, to the point where all interest is focused on what one will be able to show to friends in the future rather than the experience that one is currently living.

If this tendency can be kept in check and not become too distracting, there can be great reward in bringing some creativity into the adventure. Whether it is capturing the landscape in photography, jotting down a few notes or thoughts about a conversation you have just had or drawing a quick sketch with a pencil, such things have the potential to imprint lasting memories. With the right attitude, the desire to record your experience can make you more aware of your surroundings and more likely to give them your full attention and the necessary time.

As it was the case with planning, documenting a trip is also a way to somehow extend the journey. With planning, your research will wet your appetite as you read more and more about the places you are about to visit and, in a similar way, bringing back memories, collecting them and making use of them at a later date, will bring back some of the joys you have experienced.

Another aspect to documenting the trip refers to the way social media has transformed how we access information nowadays. Before setting off on your tour, you might well have found inspiration or valuable information in the wealth of content that is produced by people just like yourself. Completing the tour you have now become 'the expert'; experience will have taught you aspects worth sharing and, with the benefit of hindsight, you will know what could have been done differently and what worked best. The content you are willing to share can become extremely useful to others planning something similar, a rewarding thing in itself. When it comes to filming a tour it is easier when travelling with others as you can take it in turn to shoot video clips of each other both on and off the bike.

When touring on your own it becomes more challenging but it is still possible to produce an interesting video of the tour. Because variety of shots is what makes for an interesting viewing, when touring alone you will need some props to help you:

Chest Harness: This I find, is the simplest and most effective way to shoot a scenery while riding the bike. I wear the harness at all times and attach an action camera that is protruding from my chest. When I happen to ride along an interesting scene and want to record it, all that I need to do is to push a button and keep riding. Modern action cameras come with excellent stabilisation and as your body naturally absorbs some of the vibrations of the ride this is in my opinion a far better solution than mounting the camera directly on the bicycle. Having the camera at your chest level also gives an excellent first-person perspective that includes the stretched arms reaching the handlebar, resulting in a view that is not too different from the cyclist's one. The chest harness works particularly well on footage at moderate to fast speed . I use it mostly on flat roads and downhill as this is where the bicycle is at its most stable.

Selfie Stick: To give variety and a different perspective as well as the ability to film yourself as you ride, a good solution is using a Selfie Stick. The lighter and the longer the extension, the better. Of course one has to be extremely careful when using it while cycling because holding it with one hand will mean having to ride only one-handed. Vibration and stability in the footage is less of an issue when using a selfie stick. As you are filming yourself while riding, there is an optical illusion at play; the viewer focuses on the cyclist's figure and all the movements of the stick mostly go unnoticed. For this reason it is the ideal prop to use when riding slowly, particularly while climbing which often introduces a rocking motion on the bike which becomes very apparent on a chest harness clip.

Tripod: Another option to film yourself is of course offered by tripods. Some are very compact and small while other are heavier and more stable at different heights but all give the option to film you from the side of the road as you pass by. Setting up the scene is a little more distracting than the previous two as it involves preparing the tripod with smartphone or action camera, pressing the start button and then riding back and forth on the section of road that you want to film. Despite this, often the landscape around you deserves all the time you can dedicate to it in order to record it. Placing a tripod and riding towards the camera will record a view of the scenery behind you which is why it is a good idea, in scenic places, to have a look at the rear view every now and then, to assess whether stopping to film is well worth it.

Gimbal: With stabilisation advances in both smartphones and action cameras, a gimbal is not as essential but it does greatly improve the ability to shoot handheld videos that are smooth and professional, even when walking or moving.

Monetising your tour

Following what was just discussed in the previous section, and referring particularly to the aspect of social media, photography, filming, writing and podcasting are also ways to monetise your trip. This is not something that can happen immediately and it does take some time and effort, but chances are that if you are passionate about bike touring this will be effortless and feel like time well spent. For most people this probably comes naturally rather than being a choice that is made from the start. I definitely fall into this category. I never felt myself particularly talented, nor did I intentionally plan it, but with more and more experience, new ideas came to me organically.

What started simply as a way to share notes and pictures of my journeys in a blog many years ago, moved to producing videos and tutorials on how I do things and even publishing a book. Monetising this has never been my intention, but it does bring some revenue from something that I love and would do anyway. More valuable than this are the comments and support one receives, and nothing is so rewarding as those messages telling you how much your content has inspired someone to do the same. Again I try to be mindful of the fact that the travel and the experience itself should always come first.

For those extremely talented, and willing and able to put more work into it, there is of course the chance to turn this into a career. Some indeed end up earning enough money to fund a lifestyle that reflects their passion for travel and this becomes a virtuous loop where the more they travel the more they are able to put out content and make it a profession in itself. Apart from the skills, to get to this level takes patience and hard work and can only happen once you get to a high level of exposure.

This opens up new opportunities such as the chance to test equipment that is sent to you for review, or sponsorships from companies that see great value and returns in what you are able to produce. If it becomes a profession, it is likely that compromises will need to be made and there might be times when the content you need to produce determines the destination or mode of travel.

Digital content, despite its pitfalls, brings a host of new opportunities. It is also a 'great leveller' in the sense that it allows anyone to distribute content without facing the costly barriers to entry that in the past meant that only a few were able to 'make it'. A video you produce with your smartphone can today reach millions of viewers and the push of a button on a keyboard is all it takes to publish a book that can be purchased and read internationally. Of course one can argue that this is at the detriment of quality, but in the end it is the same quality that will determine whether it is appreciated and proves to be useful to many.

On the opposite side of the spectrum one could rather decide to use a tour as a way to collect funds for a charity. Many bike tours have been done with such an altruistic motive and have benefitted many associations, not only in monetary terms but also as an alternative way to spread a message or highlight a good cause.

When things go wrong

I had to resort to this generic title to discuss the possibility of things not working out exactly as one had expected. They are far too many to be more specific but what I am alluding to are things completely beyond our control. It could be a serious bike failure that cannot be fixed, getting ill in the midst of the tour, facing unexpected weather conditions and all the countless iterations of Murphy's law.

I kept this section for the end, not for it to be buried in a long index and go unnoticed, but because I kept on pushing it down my list of priorities and things that should be highlighted in a bike touring manual. Indeed it is my hope that some of the points I have shared on these pages can make a difference and help you be better prepared and prevent such events from happening in the first place. Far from wanting to dampen your enthusiasm, here are a few thoughts on how to deal with occasions when, for whatever reason, things don't quite work out as you had planned.

Such situations rarely materialise, but to be aware of their possibility will help you cope with things should they occur. For a start this awareness should point to the fact that a good way to reduce such risk is to be realistic and rather conservative in what you plan in the first place. This is a concept I have already highlighted several times, the reason being that it is an important aspect to keep in mind. When you are giving yourself some slack you are allowing that bit of flexibility that can become necessary at times. Planning a spare day or two in your schedule might make the difference between successfully completing what you set out to do or having to give up on it halfway because you had a bad day or for fear that you wouldn't make it and that time was running out. As you gain experience there might be times when you want to push yourself a little more, do something that you know will be more challenging; this is different because you know the outcome is uncertain from the start and should you not make it, it won't be seen as a failure.

Remember that 'things going wrong' is not something real you can clearly point to but rather dependent on your expectations and on something else I have mentioned before, the ability to adapt and find some alternatives. Whatever turn of events has occurred on your journey, there could be two very different outcomes. You could adapt to it, making the necessary changes in the original plan, or you could become stubborn, wanting to stick to the plan even when you know you will not make it. The former could well bring new opportunities and by the end of it you might even find out that 'things didn't really go wrong', 'things just went differently'. The latter will bring disappointment and resentment instead, which will prevent you from rescuing something that can still be appreciated and enjoyed: 'things did go wrong'.

There will be times when a positive attitude is not enough and a way around can not be found; and that is something one must accept as part of life. An Italian adventurer whom I particularly admire, once described this happening to him. He had vast experience gained in some challenging adventures like cycling through Mongolia and canoeing down the Amazon river. However, on a particular, less challenging trip in South America, he somehow felt poorly from the start. He pushed on, but his physical condition did not improve and something he had always loved to do was becoming a grind and not enjoyable anymore; hardly a week into the trip he thought it best to give up and quit. He talked about it to highlight the fact that despite good physical strength, experience and stamina, there are times when the appropriate thing to do is to stop. Yes there will be some disappointment, but you can be fine with that too and know that the next time round things will be better.

Having a folding bicycle will make the logistics of changing a plan much easier than would otherwise be the case. Whether you need a lift in a car or need to take a bus back to where you started, it will prove to be much simpler. Whenever possible one thing I would always recommend is to have a 'plan B', something else you would be able to enjoy in the event that you were forced to stop cycling. One of the reasons for the light setup I have advocated, and of carrying a backpack as part of my luggage, is that it can make you much more flexible in what you can do. Should you have to face the fact that for any reason the bike tour is not working out, you have a way to shift your focus from cycling to backpacking. Using other means of transport you are in the position to rescue a journey, making the most of it despite the situation and enjoying the places you are able to visit.

Conclusion

From here on it is for you to experiment; trying out some of the ideas I have introduced, as well as filling the gaps for what is missing or what has been left out. Any manual can only go as far as to point a direction or provide suggestions, but it is bound to fail in trying to describe all possible situations one might encounter.

I have tried to keep the content to what is most practical and useful in helping you to complete your tour, fully aware that there will be times when you will have to be resourceful and will savour the joys and rewards that come from overcoming your particular challenges.

Exploration and adventure is a way to enrich our lives, and I hope these pages will have offered some help as well as the inspiration to give it a try and see if bike touring is something that you can enjoy as much as I do. Whether this is the case or not, I hope you will keep pedalling, as even the shortest of journeys on a bicycle has a mysterious way of opening the mind and warming the heart.

❖ ❖ ❖

Resources

<u>Route Planner</u>

To get the Route Planner in Google Sheets format you will need a Google account. Follow the link below to find the document. Clicking on the Route Planner picture, or the link just below it, will open a prompt to copy the spreadsheet on your Google Drive.

http://www.bromptontraveler.com/2001/05/route-planner-google-sheets.html

<u>The Brompton Traveler on YouTube</u>

https://www.youtube.com/c/BromptonTraveler

<u>The Brompton Traveler Blog</u>

www.bromptontraveler.com

<u>The Brompton Traveler Recommended Products</u>

https://www.amazon.co.uk/shop/bromptontraveler

<u>Other books by the author</u>

Unfolding Travels (Published 2019) is available for purchase as a paperback or kindle ebook on www.amazon.com

Printed in Great Britain
by Amazon

51540757R00099